GIDE

Les Nourritures terrestres
and
La Symphonie pastorale

David H. Walker

Professor of French,
University of Keele

Grant & Cutler Ltd
1990

© Grant & Cutler Ltd 1990

ISBN 0 7293 0322 5

I.S.B.N. 84-599-3062-9

DEPÓSITO LEGAL: V. 1.387 - 1990

Printed in Spain by
Artes Gráficas Soler, S.A., Valencia
for
GRANT AND CUTLER LTD
55-57 GREAT MARLBOROUGH STREET, LONDON, W1V 2AY

Contents

Contents

Prefatory Note

Abbreviations used in this study are to the following editions of
works by Gide:

OC Oeuvres complètes d'André Gide, ed. L. Martin-Chauffier,
15 vols (Paris, Gallimard, 1932-1939).
R Romans, récits et soties, oeuvres lyriques (Paris, Gallimard,
Bibliothèque de la Pléiade, 1958).
J1 *Journal 1889-1939* (Paris, Gallimard, Bibliothèque de la Pléiade,
1948).
J2 *Journal 1939-1949, Souvenirs* (Paris, Gallimard, Bibliothèque de
la Pléiade, 1954).

Les Nourritures terrestres and *La Symphonie pastorale* are available
in paperback editions in the Folio series published by Gallimard.
I use these editions in the analysis which follows. Unless otherwise
indicated, page numbers in parentheses in section (i) of each chapter
refer to *Les Nourritures terrestres* and in section (ii) of each chapter
to *La Symphonie pastorale*. Where there is a possibility of confusion,
the former is indicated by *NT*, the latter by *SP*. References to critical
works listed in the select bibliography at the end of the volume have
an italicised number followed, if appropriate, by page number(s).

1. Introduction: a Drama in Two Acts

Twenty-one years separate the publication of *Les Nourritures terrestres* in 1897 from the writing of *La Symphonie pastorale* in 1918. Nevertheless, both works reflect Gide's constant preoccupation with related themes and experiences; and some indication of the profound affinity between them can be seen in the fact that Gide actually conceived the idea for *La Symphonie pastorale* at the time when he was planning *Les Nourritures terrestres*. It was in Toulon, in October 1893, as he was waiting to board the ship for the first of his momentous visits to North Africa, that, he tells us, he recounted to his travelling-companion 'le sujet de ce qui devint plus tard (*La*) *Symphonie pastorale*' (J2, p.523).

The decision to leave for Algeria was the culmination of several years of mental and spiritual conflict for Gide. On the one hand the young Gide was hemmed in by inhibitions and prohibitions stemming from his upbringing and background, and on the other he was troubled by the urge to sound out and liberate those impulses within him which he could not reconcile with the moral and religious codes that had presided over his adolescence. His father had died in 1880, a month before the boy's eleventh birthday, and André's mother, for all her inward insecurity and the great affection she bore her only child, adopted a rigorously puritanical and authoritarian approach to rearing him. Her religious stance was solidly protestant, and the ethical teachings she derived from her religion emphasised duty and obedience, leaving little room for the pleasures of the senses and the untoward indulgence of the appetites. The mark she and her attitudes stamped on her son was to prove indelible. During his adolescence, Gide experienced a phase of extraordinary religious fervour characterised by prayer and meditation, and quasi-monastic practices. Such tendencies were reinforced by his early love for his cousin Madeleine, a girl of similarly pious disposition with whom he was able to share his enthusiasms, both spiritual and literary: often, indeed, the two went together, since the Bible was, and would remain, an important source of inspiration in both spheres. Quotations from the Scriptures are scattered throughout his first book, *Les Cahiers d'André Walter* (1889), which Gide intended as a sort of marriage proposal to Madeleine. He dreamed, like his hero, of a marriage of souls, communing in a common adoration of God.

However, all this heavenly light inevitably cast long dark shadows. The intensity of Gide's religious ferment was in large part a reaction to the stirrings of his youthful sexuality, which troubled him greatly when his spiritual zeal faltered. His particular religious formation complicated matters, for it is in the nature of protestantism to place the responsibility for salvation directly into the hands of the individual; and in moments of turmoil, Gide had only his conscience to turn to. However, when he listened to this inner voice, he heard murmurings which were entirely out of keeping with the conventional views of his mother and their milieu. He was accustomed to conforming to patterns of behaviour which were becoming an empty appearance to him. He hoped that Madeleine would, by agreeing to marry him, sustain him against his inner demons; but she turned down his proposal on the advice of their respective families. In any case, like André Walter, the young author found that even his adoration for his cousin could not entirely supplant his other phantasms, just as the lip-service he paid to his mother's religion and morality could not stifle the voice of his instinctual revolt. Madeleine's refusal did not extinguish his determination to marry her eventually; he resolved to wait, but in the meantime he was on the horns of a dilemma. His religious upbringing exhorted him to be sincere and to follow the promptings of his inner self; but at the same time the practitioners of that same religion imposed upon him a puritan orthodoxy which left him no room for manoeuvre. At the start of 1892 he complained in his diary: 'Je m'agite dans ce dilemme: être moral; être sincère. La morale consiste à supplanter l'être naturel (le vieil homme) par un être factice préféré. Mais alors, on n'est plus sincère. Le vieil homme, c'est l'homme sincère' (J1, pp.29-30).

The struggle to reconcile these opposing exigencies or to rise above the conflict in the service of art and the ideal is reflected in the works of 1890 to 1893: *Le Traité du Narcisse*, *Le Voyage d'Urien*, *La Tentative amoureuse*. Ultimately, however, Gide saw that for literary as well as personal reasons, he needed an escape route. His divided personality was wilting into languor, melancholy and fruitless introspection; drawn as he was by his intimate problems to the idealist, Mallarmé-inspired school of symbolist writing, his literary output was in danger of becoming ever more ethereal and evanescent in style. By 1893 his mind was made up, and he determined on a journey to exotic North Africa, inwardly declaring, 'Au nom de quel Dieu, de quel idéal me défendez-vous de vivre selon ma nature? Et cette nature, où m'entraînerait-elle, si simplement je la suivais?' (J2, p.550). In a different climate, amidst a different culture, perhaps he would find a way out of his inner conflict: 'J'entrevis enfin que ce dualisme discordant pourrait peut-être bien se résoudre en une harmonie' (ibid.).

Gide was to devote most of the next three years to travel, spending three extended spells in Algeria and chronicling in *Les Nourritures terrestres* the life-changing impact of his journeys. In the winter and spring of 1893-94 he fell ill and in the oasis town of Biskra underwent a 'convalescence merveilleuse': 'Je renaquis avec un être neuf, sous un ciel neuf et au milieu de choses complètement renouvelées', he writes (*NT*, p.28). His senses, sharpened by illness and by the strangeness of a foreign land, brought home to him the sheer physical delight of abandoning thought and existing solely through the body: 'Tandis que se volatilisait tout vouloir, je laissais les sensations, en moi poreux comme une ruche, secrètement distiller ce miel qui coula dans mes *Nourritures*' (J2, p.575). The idea for this book came to him with his virtual rebirth, and he allowed it to write itself, as he put it (J2, p.574), over the following two or three years. In letters, notebooks and diaries he described his experiences, jotting down incidents and sensations as they occurred, evolving a literary form capable of conveying the character of this primal response to nature that he was discovering within him. 'Il faut précipiter la littérature dans un abîme de sensualisme d'où elle ne puisse sortir que complètement régénérée,' he declared in a letter to a friend (quoted in *18*, p.22).

On his return to France and the 'pluvieuse terre de Normandie' where the family's estate and farm of La Roque were situated (*NT*, p.94), doctors advised him that mountain air would help his lungs recover from the tuberculosis that had infected them. Thus it came about that he spent the winter of 1894 in Switzerland, at La Brévine, a 'vilain trou' as he called it in a letter to his mother (*6*, II, p.376). The village later became the setting for *La Symphonie pastorale*. For Gide this period was a plunge back into an extreme version of the joyless existence he had just begun to break away from. He conceived an abiding distaste for the people and the region, holding them ever afterwards — without justification, as Jean Delay points out[1] — to be inhospitable and imbued with 'une sorte de morosité et de rigidité calviniste' (J2, p.579). Here was the perfect contrast to his new outlook on life: and something of this incompatibility between idyllic inner vision and austere environment informs the irony in *La Symphonie pastorale*.

Early in 1895 Gide returned to Algeria. If the first visit had led to his discovery of the life of the senses, the second visit took the form of a specifically sexual awakening. He met Oscar Wilde, then at the height of his fame prior to his disastrous downfall in the trials of May 1895. Gide had earlier met Wilde in Paris and Italy; but now the celebrated aesthete was recklessly indulging his homosexual inclinations among the Arab boys, and encouraged Gide to do the same. The ecstasy Gide experienced banished the last of his uncertainties. Here, it seemed to him, lay his true nature, the source of enduring joy for him. This was the crucial step in his life; and it contributes in no small measure to the erotic charge of the lyricism in *Les Nourritures terrestres*. Moreover, it also accounts for the

---

[1] See *6*, II, pp.380-81. The local pastor made Gide very welcome, in fact — and was rewarded for his pains, twenty-five years later, by malicious gossip on the part of parishioners who thought *La Symphonie pastorale* was the story of events that actually happened at La Brévine.

character of Ménalque, the emancipated mentor who initiates the book's narrator much as Wilde influenced Gide.

Strengthened in his senses, confirmed in his sexuality, Gide adopted a more explicitly rebellious attitude towards the forces which had weighed on his life up to then. Chief among these, of course, was his mother, whose over-solicitous concern for his well-being had long been a source of friction between her and her son. Already in the previous year, alarmed at the news of his illness and arriving unannounced in person, she had disrupted a promising *ménage à trois* which Gide and his travelling-companion had established with an Arab girl. (It may be that this traumatic interruption of his heterosexual apprenticeship actually contributed to his subsequent homosexual option.) Now she perceived a new tone in her son's letters, became fearful of his intentions and began to deluge him with directives — about his plan to buy land in Algeria and build a house there, about his wish to bring an Arab boy back to France with him, about the title of *Les Nourritures terrestres*, which seemed to her to augur no good at all for the book's eventual contents. Gide refused to submit to her horrified recommendations, making it clear that the days when he accepted restrictions, observed taboos and respected authority were well and truly over. The best Madame Gide and he could achieve was an uneasy compromise.

However, Madame Gide died suddenly soon after her son's return to France, in May 1895. It was the moment of truth for Gide. He was compelled to recognise that a large part of his nature, and even his fledgling revolt itself, depended for their substance on what she represented. Stricken by grief and a profound sense of disorientation as an abyss opened up in his life, he proposed once more to Madeleine, who accepted him. The couple were married in October, after Gide had been assured by a doctor from whom he sought advice that his homosexual tendencies would disappear of their own accord once he became a husband. He had found a new anchor. But by subconsciously casting Madeleine in the role vacated by his mother, he was merely inaugurating the second act in the drama which was to reach its climax in the events surrounding the creation of *La Symphonie pastorale*.

The marriage began with an intention on Gide's part to open Madeleine's eyes to the joys of travel and emancipation: the couple set out on a honeymoon journey which would take in Switzerland, Italy and North Africa. But it did not live up to Gide's expectations. He was unable to consummate the marriage: his relatively untested heterosexual drives proved incapable of coping with the great veneration in which he held Madeleine both for herself and as the embodiment of a certain forbidding image of woman he had inherited from his mother. The 'Récit de Ménalque', a keynote section which opens the fourth book of *Les Nourritures terrestres*, was written during the honeymoon, in November 1895: it may have been the result of a compensatory mechanism, an attempt on Gide's part to overcome the humiliation of his marriage by giving free rein to the impulses which were unable to find satisfaction (see *28* and *29*). Whatever the facts of the matter were, it does seem clear that Gide had to acknowledge that his yearning for the company of boys had not subsided. Moreover, the presence of Madeleine was obviously incompatible with this yearning. A brief section of dialogue in *Les Nourritures terrestres* appears to reflect something of the situation prevailing between the newly-weds. The narrator enthuses over the spectacle of children coming out of school; Angèle (a slightly ironic pseudonym Gide used in several works for characters connected with Madeleine) comments, 'Cela ne suffit pas pour faire une poésie'; whereupon the narrator retorts: 'Alors, laissons cela' (*NT*, p.97).

In spite of this area of their marriage where silence seems to have been the rule, by the time *Les Nourritures terrestres* was completed in late 1896, the couple had settled relatively happily into a pattern their relationship would follow for the next twenty years. So Gide could later write with a certain justification: 'J'écrivais ce livre au moment où, par le mariage, je venais de fixer ma vie; où j'aliénais volontairement une liberté que mon livre, oeuvre d'art, revendiquait aussitôt d'autant plus' (*NT*, p.11). Nevertheless, his renunciation of freedom was far from entire; nor were his desires to be satisfied by the purely artistic pursuit of fulfilment. The couple appear to have come to a tacit agreement that Gide's life henceforth would have two centres. At one pole was Madeleine, the image of spirituality and selflessness, all that Gide had aspired to as a young man and would continue to adore, in his idiosyncratic way, throughout his life; at the other were Gide's sexual impulses, his anti-conformist, anti-authoritarian urges. This dichotomy was to nourish almost the whole of Gide's ensuing creative work, emerging with particular clarity in the contrast between *L'Immoraliste* (1902), the account of a man's implacable quest for self-fulfilment, and *La Porte étroite* (1909), the story of a young woman's pious abnegation and unremitting self-sacrifice.

By the time he wrote these works and perfected his technique of the *récit*, or first-person narrative, Gide's examination of the issues thrown up by the explosion of *Les Nourritures* had crystallised into a critique of orthodoxy and of doctrinaire attitudes in general. And ironically it was a cornerstone of protestant theology that had permitted Gide's radical views. The full implications of the protestant's freedom of conscience had begun to dawn on him in 1894, in Switzerland, as he mused over theological questions in an environment and a frame of mind he was to re-create in *La Symphonie pastorale*;[2] and in 1896 he published on the subject a short essay called 'Morale chrétienne' he had written while composing *Les Nourritures terrestres*. In it he quotes an article by Faguet:

> N'y ayant pas de limite au libre examen, le protestantisme créait une religion illimitée, donc indéfinie, donc indéfinissable, qui ne saurait pas, le jour où le libre examen lui apporterait l'athéisme, si l'athéisme fait partie d'elle-même ou non ... (J1, p.95)

---

[2] Compare Gide's letter to his mother, 22 September 1894: 'Quand Luther proclama le libre examen, des puissances dans l'ombre ont dû rire' (quoted in *6*, II, pp.365-66). Delay stresses the parallel between the views expressed in the letters and diaries of this period and those later set down in *La Symphonie*.

The logical product of freedom of conscience, then, was the free-thinker: and Gide followed this logic through. Up to the time of his emancipation, the Bible had been a daily source of succour; he had found in it the strength to struggle against his nature, and menaces to encourage him in the fight. Now, using the protestant prerogative of free interpretation of the Scriptures in the light of his new outlook, he rejected the principle of authority and sought to reinstate Christ's message of the Gospels in all its subversive power, seeing in it a corroboration of the message he was seeking to communicate in *Les Nourritures terrestres*:

> Je m'étonne que le protestantisme, en repoussant les hiérarchies de l'Eglise, n'ait pas repoussé du même coup les oppressantes institutions de Saint Paul, le dogmatisme de ses épîtres, pour ne relever plus que des seuls Evangiles. On en viendra bientôt, je pense, à dégager les paroles du Christ, pour les laisser paraître plus émancipatrices qu'elles ne le paraissent jusqu'alors.
> (J1, p.96)

When this happens, argues Gide, people will find in the Gospels an attack on the family, the rejection of possessions and material security, and an incitement to just the free-wheeling life-style he was preaching in *Les Nourritures terrestres*: 'O avènement de cet "état nomade", toute mon âme te souhaite!', he writes.

Such an approach to religion and the Scriptures was to be a constant of Gide's life, and clearly underlies the ideas put forward by the pastor in *La Symphonie pastorale*. *Le Retour de l'enfant prodigue*, Gide's 1907 reformulation of the Gospel parable, also anticipates the later work. In this unorthodox adaptation, the prodigal son's return does not mark the moral bankruptcy of the vagabond life-style, since he incites a younger brother to leave home in his turn. Equally important, the Elder Brother, the embodiment of the Church hierarchies which claim to speak for the Father and which deal severely with doctrinal deviants, is rebuked by the Father who maintains that each individual must be free to seek Him in his own way.

In 1910 Gide made notes for a preface to *La Symphonie pastorale*, which at this time he intended to call *L'Aveugle* and which, of course, he was not actually to write for another eight years. The purpose of this preface was to restate Gide's view that Saint Paul, Calvin, and all the religious institutions deriving from them, catholic and protestant alike, ran counter to the spirit of the Gospels. 'Mon christianisme ne relève que du Christ', he declares (J1, p.300), a position ringingly reaffirmed in 1912: 'Le catholicisme est inadmissible. Le protestantisme est intolérable. Et je me sens profondément chrétien' (J1, p.367).

Gide's radical approach to religion, paralleling his critical perspective on all other conformisms, therefore develops directly from the era of *Les Nourritures*. His refusal to align himself with any fixed scheme of values culminated, in 1914, in the comic epic *Les Caves du Vatican*, which lambasts a whole host of what it terms *crustacés* — individuals whose lives have ossified into the conventional patterns of the bourgeois, the priest, the scientist, the novelist, but also the stereotype atheist or moral rebel. Gide's own unrelenting insistence on sincerity kept him free of the pitfalls of weakness or hypocrisy into which his characters stumbled.

Or so it seemed before the outbreak of World War One. However, the next four years were to be a period of turmoil which called into question the entire edifice of Gide's life and thought. He worked in a centre for war refugees, and found himself succumbing to a contagion of despair and demoralisation. All around him it seemed that friends and colleagues were turning to religion, and principally the Catholic Church, for moral sustenance and an escape from uncertainty. Gide himself had flirted with catholicism: he had been fascinated by the truculent fervour of the poet Paul Claudel who had tried to convert him. It had disturbed him only slightly when Claudel, horrified by the homosexual implications of a passage which Gide refused to cut from *Les Caves du Vatican*, more or less consigned him to hell. But early in 1916 Gide received a letter from his friend Henri Ghéon announcing his conversion. Ghéon had been very close to Gide: he had the same homosexual inclinations and had accompanied Gide on many a furtive escapade in search of adolescent partners. Hence the news of his renunciation came as a severe blow. It triggered off for Gide a period of intense guilt, self-doubt and even self-loathing.

He turned, as ever, to the Scriptures, recording his meditations in a notebook he entitled *Numquid et tu..?*, after the words addressed to Nicodemus in John 7. 52, challenging him to assert his allegiance to Christ. Gide pondered the Gospels in search of an answer to his anguish; while he sought solace in his despair, he can also be seen on occasion striving to justify, through a personal interpretation of Christ's words, both his sexual proclivities and his longing for happiness. These traits he would later attribute to his fictional pastor: and indeed we find extracts from *Numquid et tu..?* transcribed in *La Symphonie pastorale* — adapted into the form of a dialogue which graphically illustrates the extent to which Gide is capable in his fiction of distancing himself from his most intimate concerns while using them as the stuff of his art (see chapter 3).

At the same time, in early 1916 Gide began to write his autobiography *Si le grain ne meurt*: and it was gradually borne in upon him, as he relived his childhood in the light of intervening events, that his so-called liberation had not been all he had considered it to be. He had duped himself, in believing he could accommodate earlier influences within a more radical way of life. This sensation became so acute that he wondered frequently whether the inner voice whose words he had heeded as a young man was not, in fact, as his catholic acquaintances affirmed, merely the expression of an inner demon. At all events, he had freed himself from orthodox morality only to discover that the so-called sincerity in whose name he had broken away brought its own dangers in the form of the manifold self-delusions the human mind is prone to. And Madeleine, who had virtually taken over from his mother as the representative of propriety and purity in his life, stood as a living reproach for his conduct. The struggle to reconcile once more the urgings of his instincts with fidelity to Madeleine, and the guilt generated by this inner strife, plunged Gide into a grave emotional crisis in mid-1916.

We have very few details as to what occurred between Gide and his wife — he destroyed the section of his diary covering this phase — but the period saw the beginning of a marked deterioration in their relationship (see J1, pp.566-67, 569; *13*, pp.332-55; *37*, p.1xxiv). The love which had been a source of inspiration for the author he came to view as an inhibiting factor and a threat to the fulfilment of his creative vocation.

Confronted once more by moral and religious questions of the kind that had haunted his youth, Gide was in a sense renewing the experience which had preceded *Les Nourritures terrestres*. Matters came to a head in May 1917, when Gide fell in love with Marc Allégret, the son of Pastor Elie Allégret who was a long-standing friend of the Gide family. Up to this time Gide's homosexual partners had not really been rivals of Madeleine; he always maintained that his heart and soul were entirely hers, even though he had to go elsewhere for satisfaction of his senses. But his love for Marc represented a true infidelity to his wife; it was a love of his entire being, he felt — and it left little room for her. Moreover, despite Gide's attempts to dissemble, Madeleine soon sensed that something was amiss:[3] and the extent of her husband's betrayal was made brutally clear to her in December 1917 when she chanced upon a letter from Ghéon remonstrating with Gide for his past turpitudes and beseeching him to abandon the sinful *affaire* on which, he said, he could tell that Gide had embarked from the elated tone of his recent letters.[4] The couple never discussed the situation candidly, but

---

[3] Madeleine later told Gide the precise date when her situation became intolerable: it coincided exactly with the beginning of the *affaire*. 'Je suis confondu de sa force de pénétration', he commented when reporting this to Maria Van Rysselberghe. See her *Les Cahiers de la Petite Dame*, I (*Cahiers André Gide*, IV, 1973), p.12.

[4] Jean Schlumberger's record of the account Gide gave him suggests January 1916 as the date of this incident: see *Madeleine et André Gide* (Paris, Gallimard, 1956), pp.179-200. However, it is a letter dated 13 December 1917 which seems the only one likely to have brought about such a revelation: see André Gide-Henri Ghéon, *Correspondance*, 2 vols (Paris, Gallimard, 1976), vol.I, pp.929-32. Gide published his intimate diary reflecting his and his wife's difficulties, along with a self-incriminating obituary, after Madeleine's death in 1938: *Et nunc manet in te*, J2, p.1141.

a gulf had opened between them. By now Gide seems to have decided that his personality had irredeemably outgrown his marriage in certain important respects, and that Madeleine could not furnish him with the renewal of artistic inspiration he needed.

The story had come full circle. Just as, some twenty years previously, he had fought off the influence of his mother in the first flush of homosexual experience, so now he was impelled to override his scruples and put behind him the pious respectability that Madeleine stood for. 'La pensée de [Marc] me maintient dans un état constant de lyrisme que je ne connaissais plus depuis mes *Nourritures*', he wrote in his diary (J1, p.641). As if to commemorate the parallel with the era of the earlier book, Gide began to compose a sequel, *Les Nouvelles Nourritures*. The completed work was not to see the light of day until 1935 — and then in a form much altered from its original inspiration by Gide's political involvements: nonetheless, there flows into *La Symphonie pastorale* a current of lyricism stemming directly from this resurgence of the fervour that lay behind *Les Nourritures terrestres*.

Once again, therefore, Gide's instinctive impulses brought him into conflict with conventional morality and family relationships. An atmosphere of disruption and mute estrangement reigned in the Gide marriage. Simultaneously, Gide's involvement with Marc was by its nature incompatible with a proper respect for the authority of the boy's family, while his status as a friend of the Allégrets meant that the intimate events of the minister's domestic life were relayed to him by both sides. At this time Pastor Allégret's household was itself in a state of smouldering crisis. The pastor's frequent absences on missionary work evidently made him unaware of his children's needs and his own neglect of them; rifts were developing within his home as the oppressive protestant morality it rested on began to degenerate into conflict and resentment between the children and the parents. The parallels between this situation and the drama Gide himself had undergone as a young man were all the more telling for the writer in that Gide was engaged at precisely the same period in describing his own youthful traumas in his memoirs. Clearly *La Symphonie pastorale* was affected by this coincidence: Gide has derived the domestic background to his *récit* from the Allégret household,[5] grafting a transposed version of his own marital infidelity on to the original and adding to it a reflection of the strained relations between husband and wife that prevailed in his marriage at the time.

Gide began writing *La Symphonie pastorale* in February 1918. The *récit* thus shares with *Les Nourritures terrestres* the distinction of having been written at the same time as the author was living out the events it is based on (see *40*). Gide even interrupted his writing to go off for four months in England with Marc. (Martin's examination of the manuscripts permitted him to fix the break at what is page 103 of the Folio edition: see *37*, p.xciv.) He left behind a cruel letter to Madeleine in which he explained bluntly that he had to get away from her for the sake of his creative powers. When he returned home to complete the novel late in 1918, he was unaware that in his absence Madeleine had broken a precious link with the past that bound them together. The atmosphere of desolation evoked in the closing lines of *La Symphonie pastorale* was to prove but a foretaste of the emotional agonies he underwent on discovering the truth. 'Ma *Symphonie pastorale* (la Jeune Aveugle) est achevée depuis hier', he wrote in a letter of 19 November 1918.[6] On 21 November his diary entry began: 'Madeleine a détruit toutes mes lettres' (J2, p.1145). This unique testimony of his love for her, going back to the spiritual exaltation of their youth, represented for Gide an essential figure in the pattern of his life. Though in later years the couple did retrieve elements of the former harmony that united them, neither fully recovered from the moral mutilation which was the price of Gide's *disponibilité*.

---

[5] Gide's virtual obsession with the Allégret household during and after the writing of *La Symphonie pastorale* is repeatedly remarked on in *Les Cahiers de la Petite Dame*, op.cit., pp.13, 26, 30, 240-42, etc. Claude Martin sees Mme Elie Allégret as one source for Amélie, and points out that Gide reduced the number of his pastor's children from six to five in order, perhaps, to avoid too glaring a parallel (*37*, p.xciv). The Allégrets later served as the model for the Vedel-Azaïs family in *Les Faux-Monnayeurs*.

[6] Letter to Dorothy Bussy, 19 November 1918; André Gide-Dorothy Bussy, *Correspondance*, I (*Cahiers André Gide*, IX, Paris, Gallimard, 1979), p.101.

The particular significance of the background to Gide's fiction can be seen from the preceding brief excursion into it. Through the irony inherent in the author's use of first-person narrative, Gide's art constantly reveals him transforming his experience into models of severe self-scrutiny which raise moral, psychological and aesthetic questions of general and enduring urgency. In the context of the present study, however, biographical analysis serves to underline some of the elements that link *Les Nourritures terrestres* and *La Symphonie pastorale*. In the rest of my discussion I shall consider the texts largely as literary artefacts that generate meanings independently of their sources in the author's life: but before we abandon the background to these books, one more common thread is worthy of mention.

Gide altered the original title of *L'Aveugle* to *La Symphonie pastorale*, for reasons about which it may be fruitful to speculate. One result of this change (though not necessarily a reason for it) was to recall *Les Nourritures terrestres* via a subtle play on words which is characteristic of the author of *Le Voyage d'Urien* and *Les Caves du Vatican*. Gide had summed up the doctrine of the earlier text, which has a good deal in common with the views of the pastor, in the term *nomadisme*. He indicated the significance of this word in a pre-publication version of the 'Récit de Ménalque' which contains the line: 'L'Evangile y mène... On appellera ta doctrine Nomadisme, du beau mot *nomos*, pâturage' (see *27*; *OC* II, p.viii). Hence the *nourritures terrestres* of the title are associated with the pastoral life — taking the term in the sense it derives from its Greek etymological root: the nomad wanders through the world in search of new nourishment, new pastures. On the other hand, *La Symphonie pastorale* echoes this idea of a pastoral idyll while combining it with an allusion to the minister who follows Christ's injunction: 'Pais mes brebis' (John 21. 15-17). Thus the two titles overlap; both books project an idyllic vision of nature and preach sermons, as it were, on the various types of nourishment available to humankind.

2. The Pedagogical Complex

(i)

A characteristic feature of *Les Nourritures terrestres* is the book's striking form of address: '*Ne te méprends pas, Nathanaël...*' From the opening lines, the reader is hailed, so to speak, in a subtly ambivalent manner. The explicit vocative, the *tutoiement*, appeals to the reader's individual personality, inviting him or her to participate in an experience conducted in an atmosphere of intimacy and friendliness; but the name Nathanaël, accompanied as it frequently is by the imperative, points to the author's attempt to impose a pattern of behaviour and an identity of his own making upon the reader. The 'tu' whom the book addresses is in theory open to anyone to fill; but in practice Nathanaël is not just any reader (for one thing he is male). He is a character defined for specific purposes by the text; and to identify with Nathanaël, to become the 'tu' of *Les Nourritures*, the reader must be prepared to adopt a certain stance while actually reading. *Les Nourritures terrestres* does explicitly what most texts do implicitly: it constructs a narratee, a 'reader in the text',[7] appealing to certain aspects of the actual reader's experience and inviting him or her to set aside the rest.

The opening book develops this invitation in a particular way, establishing the status of the narrator, the supposed character of Nathanaël, and the nature of the relationship between the two. The narrator is a person who possesses knowledge, the fruit of experience: he speaks in aphorisms and lapidary statements of truth

---

[7] See Susan R. Suleiman, Inge Crosman, eds, *The Reader in the Text. Essays on Audience and Interpretation* (New Jersey, Princeton University Press, 1980); Shlomith Rimmon-Kenan, *Narrative Fiction: Contemporary Poetics*, New Accents (London, Methuen, 1983), pp.86-89, 103-05.

— 'Chaque créature indique Dieu, aucune ne le révèle' (p.19) — interspersed with references to the adventures that have led him to this wisdom: 'Tandis que d'autres publient ou travaillent, j'ai passé trois années de voyage à oublier au contraire tout ce que j'avais appris par la tête' (p.19). Nathanaël, by contrast, is in a state of relative ignorance and inexperience: 'Tu ne sauras jamais...' (p.19). We have here the essence of a pedagogical relationship; the expert addresses the novice, whom he establishes as a novice by reminding him of his need for enlightenment and confronting him with authoritative utterances and insights. Then, by a deft manipulation of pronouns, he moves to bridge this gap between them: 'L'incertitude de nos voies nous tourmenta toute la vie. Que te dirais-je? Tout choix est effrayant, quand on y songe ... Nous croyons tous devoir découvrir Dieu' (p.20). The 'nous' and 'on' evoke a common experience, one that can be shared — one that has been undergone by the narrator and which he can help Nathanaël to cope with. The narrator reminds Nathanaël of the young man's uncertainties and fears, as it were, the better to present himself as a guide and mentor. He has known the wretchedness of the youth who is unsure of his way in life — 'Les premiers jours de douteuse extase passés ... ce fut une période inquiète d'attente et comme une traversée de marais' (p.25) — and offers to help Nathanaël escape from a 'ténébreuse ... jeunesse' (p.152). The narrator exploits a mixture of intimidation — warning the adolescent Nathanaël of the ordeals that await him — , commiseration — underlining sympathetically the apprehension and uncertainties he is currently a prey to —, and reassurance — pointing to the fact that he, the narrator, has recovered from his malady. But while he offers reassurance and the possibility of an escape for the young man, the narrator is still holding something back. The core of his emancipation and a considerable part of his teachings seem to have resulted from his acquaintance with Ménalque, and his all too brief allusions to this (e.g. pp.20, 24, 25) shroud matters in an air of mystery. What, indeed, has he learned from Ménalque?

Tu ne m'as pas enseigné la sagesse, Ménalque. Pas la sagesse, mais l'amour.

J'eus pour Ménalque plus que de l'amitié, Nathanaël, et à peine moins que de l'amour. Je l'aimais aussi comme un frère. (p.23)

The essential element in this seems to be the special relationship between the two. And it is the nature of this relationship, as much as any doctrine, which the narrator is intent on passing on to Nathanaël. In any case, the important issues cannot be taught: 'Tout ce que tu gardes en toi de connaissances *distinctes* restera distinct de toi jusques à la consommation des siècles. Pourquoi y attaches-tu tant de prix?' (p.21). What matters is what is lived, but the evocation of Ménalque brings with it suggestions of a special kind of living. What emerges, then, in *Les Nourritures terrestres*, is not so much a simple didactic tone — in any case, most of the verbs referring to teaching are in the future tense, offering the prospect, not the reality, of knowledge — as a proselytising one. The narrator is concerned with converting Nathanaël to a way of life which will generate, in appropriate forms, the knowledge he needs. Clearly the narrator has been initiated by Ménalque, and in part his purpose is to portray his experience as acolyte of this particular mentor in order that he in turn might graduate to the status of mentor, with Nathanaël as his own acolyte. Two features are significant here. One is that by evoking Ménalque, the narrator lends weight to his own utterances: 'Formes diverses de la vie; toutes vous me parûtes belles. (Ce que je te dis là, c'est ce que me disait Ménalque)' (p.24). Another is that by situating the source of wisdom in another figure, the narrator reinforces the remoteness and mystery of his teachings, as if they are an arcane secret accessible only via certain initiatory practices to which he alone holds the key. The enigmatic relationship the narrator remembers confers on Ménalque a status compounded of these two elements. The narrator evidently envies Ménalque's authority ('Si j'étais Ménalque, pour te conduire j'aurais pris ta main droite...', p.15), and needs allusions to his predecessor in order to buttress his own invocations to Nathanaël or to ratify his more daring pronouncements: 'J'espère bien avoir connu toutes les passions et tous les vices; au moins les ai-je favorisés ... — me disait encore Ménalque' (p.24). But at the same time Ménalque inspires an admiration mingled with the fear and disapproval that attend on controversial characters:

> Ménalque est dangereux; crains-le; il se fait réprouver
> par les sages, mais ne se fait pas craindre par les
> enfants... il rend leur coeur malade d'un désir d'aigres
> fruits sauvages et soucieux d'étrange amour. (pp.23-24)

This again imbues the book's message with a special kind of glamour. It constitutes a challenge, it flies in the face of conventional wisdom, but appeals to an élite possessed of certain specifically childlike qualities. The authority of the pedagogue combines with the charisma of the guru who conveys special kinds of knowledge to a privileged few. Thus initiation and seduction go hand in hand as the book proceeds:

> Nathanaël, j'aimerais te donner une joie que ne t'aurait
> donnée encore aucun autre ... Je voudrais m'adresser à
> toi plus intimement que ne l'a fait encore aucun autre.
> (p.22)

> Nathanaël, je veux enflammer tes lèvres d'une soif
> nouvelle, et puis approcher d'elles des coupes pleines de
> fraîcheur. J'ai bu; je sais les sources où les lèvres se
> désaltèrent. (p.112)

The allusive quality of so much that the narrator says enhances the fervour of the prospective acolyte. Is he really talking about springs, or is that a symbol of something else? What exactly is the 'joy' of which he speaks? The rhetoric requires the complicity of the reader — but the reader readily accords this complicity, for fear of excluding himself from the sort of élite which the narrator carefully hints at, by means of a 'nous' here and there, strategically situated in the text (e.g. pp. 65, 142). Such devices as these, combined with the celebration of 'attentes' (pp.26-29) and 'départs' (p.37), seem designed to provoke in the reader an impatience to know, to enter into the narrator's secrets.

Thus the reader who takes up the position designated by the name Nathanaël is rendered particularly susceptible to the attractions of the exotic landscapes, the sumptuous perceptions and sophisticated experiences which the narrator parades before him. The panoramas that unfold in *Les Nourritures terrestres* form the alluring backdrop to an equally seductive array of exhortations, maxims, aphorisms, and other pseudo-moral formulae. The gist of these precepts is that Nathanaël should abandon the restrictive categories imposed by reason, convention and society and make himself available to all the impulses and sensations that will ensue: 'désir', 'amour', 'ferveur' and 'disponibilité' are keywords which resound throughout the volume. What they have in common is that they are anti-intellectual, calling for an enhanced response to physical existence, a heightened sensuality and sensibility — and a further degree of suggestibility in the face of the narrator's blandishments.

As models or practical ideals, the text returns repeatedly to exemplars of the relationship between an older and a younger man. Ménalque and the narrator, Ménalque and the schoolboy he abducts (p.67), the poet Hafiz and his cup-bearer (p.124), the narrator and his various encounters with shepherd boys, children and vagabonds (pp.52, 94-96, 137-38, 139-40), all mirror, in a sense, the narrator's interest in Nathanaël. And indeed, the tone of the narrator's invocations often betrays something more than a merely pedagogical motivation: the insistently repeated 'je voudrais' in the paragraph that ends 'Je voudrais m'approcher de toi et que tu *m'aimes*' (p.22) is symptomatic of the sort of desires which emerge with even greater force in Book Two:

> Nathanaël! ... je voudrais ... m'étendre sur toi tout entier, ma bouche sur ta bouche, et mon front sur ton front, tes

> mains froides dans mes mains brûlantes ... afin que dans
> la volupté tu t'éveilles. (p.44)

Is this to say, then, that the text is a cynical manipulation of the reader aimed at permitting Gide to indulge his pederastic fantasies, as has been argued by hostile critics, and eminent figures who in later life came to resent the spell Gide's text had worked on them in their youth?[8] The occasional admission appears to suggest as much:

> Certes, il m'a plu souvent qu'une doctrine et même qu'un
> système complet de pensées ordonnées justifiât à moi-
> même mes actes; mais parfois je ne l'ai plus pu
> considérer que comme l'abri de ma sensualité. (p.43)

What is beyond doubt is that for Gide the book 'impliquait une théorie de vie que le lyrisme seul ne suffisait pas à montrer' and that the device of addressing the text to Nathanaël was intended to permit the tacit message to emerge in the guise of 'le besoin de prosélytisme' (5, 30, p.28). However, this erotic proselytism has a broad relevance. There is, of course, a long tradition, going back at least to Ancient Greece, that stresses the beneficent effect on a young man of the affectionate attentions of an elder; Gide makes much of such traditions in *Corydon* (1911-18), his treatise on homosexuality. But the wider reference of *Les Nourritures terrestres* is sexuality in general, that libido which Freud was to place at the centre of human activity. And it is this life-enhancing energy in its undifferentiated form that Gide is striving to liberate, 'afin que dans la volupté tu t'éveilles — *puis me laisses*', as he writes. Gide does not seek sexual possession of Nathanaël; rather he seeks to initiate him into 'volupté', sensual pleasure that for him is the cornerstone of life in all its forms. 'Chaque action parfaite s'accompagne de volupté' (p.38), he writes, and elsewhere he insists:

---

[8] See for example Jacques Vier, *Gide* (Paris, Desclée de Brouwer, 1970), p.64; Pierre Emmanuel, quoted in *20*, pp.242-44; François Mauriac, in *Gide-Mauriac, Correspondance* (*Cahiers André Gide*, II, Paris, Gallimard, 1971), pp.128-30; Marcel Drouin, quoted in *28*, p.427.

> Volupté! Ce mot, je voudrais le redire sans cesse; je le
> voudrais synonyme de *bien-être*, et même qu'il suffît de
> dire *être*, simplement. (p.49)

An important aspect of *Les Nourritures terrestres* is its concern to
teach the reader how to sharpen his senses, revivify his powers of
perception and set aside his intellect in favour of pure sensation.
Nathanaël will thereby open himself to a truer communion with, and
understanding of, the natural world. But here too, in the final
analysis, the message is the same:

> ...émerveillons-nous à présent de ceci: chaque fécon-
> dation s'accompagne de volupté. Le fruit s'enveloppe de
> saveur; et de plaisir toute persévérance à la vie.
> (pp.105-06)

Such statements explain the 'volupté' which suffuses Gide's
evocations of nature: phrases such as 'amoureuse beauté de la terre...
paysage où mon désir s'est enfoncé' (p.32) are typical products of his
lyricism. But the erotic charge at the core of his inspiration has a
polymorphous quality which enables it to extend to all manner of
desires and appetites, taking in the whole of existence:

> devant chaque source m'attendait une soif ... — et
> j'aurais voulu d'autres mots pour marquer mes autres
> désirs
>> de marche, où s'ouvrait une route;
>> de repos, où l'ombre invitait;
>> de nage, au bord des eaux profondes;
>> d'amour ou de sommeil au bord de chaque lit. (p.33)

In a pre-permissive age, when pleasure was only one remove from
downright immorality, Gide was already being subversive simply by
suggesting that pleasure should be the basis of education and living.
At the same time, he is proposing a conception of 'volupté' which
embraces both erotic connotations and the diverse manifestations

and sublimations of which sexual energy is capable. For pleasure as an awakening to life can be a mark of freedom: it defies categorisation and conditioning and thus leads the way to a far-reaching emancipation. When Herbert Marcuse, a guru among the social and sexual revolutionaries of the 1960s, wrote his book *Eros and Civilisation*, he was in a sense following a trail blazed by *Les Nourritures terrestres* — as were subsequent critical theorists such as Roland Barthes who have come to see pleasure as a crucial ideological issue. Both Ménalque and the narrator offer an apprenticeship in pleasure which has emancipation as its overriding objective, as can be seen in the 'anguish of freedom' which is Ménalque's chief legacy: 'Ah! Ménalque, avec toi j'aurais voulu courir encore sur d'autres routes. Mais tu haïssais la faiblesse et prétendais m'apprendre à te quitter' (p.24).

Ultimately, the only pedagogy that is mutually beneficial to both teacher and taught is that which leaves each free to go his own way: '*Nathanaël, à présent, jette mon livre. Emancipe-t'en. ...Eduquer! — Qui donc éduquerais-je, que moi-même?*' (p.163). For all the seductive rhetoric of Gide's writing, *Les Nourritures terrestres* offers an education which avoids the pitfalls of tutelage and leads, instead, to 'délivrance', as Gide considered all education should (J1, p.636).

(ii)

'Je m'étais fait tout un roman de l'éducation de Gertrude,' says the narrator of *La Symphonie pastorale*, thus situating his narrative within the tradition of novels of education such as Rousseau's *Emile*, 'et la réalité me forçait par trop d'en rabattre' (pp.31-32). This juxtaposition of an ideal pedagogical process and the considerably less satisfying reality of the practical teaching experience sums up an important aspect of the novel's thematic substance. Almost from the outset the pastor's undertaking is envisaged systematically, and is grounded in proven practice: the story of Laura Bridgeman which inspired Dickens's *The Cricket on the Hearth* provides a practical model to follow. In addition, the pastor takes the advice of Dr

Martins and draws his inspiration from the classic premises of the eighteenth-century philosopher Condillac (p.34) who used the metaphor of a 'statue animée', a statue with sense perceptions, to illustrate his thesis that knowledge derives solely from the accumulation of sense impressions. However, in spite of the pastor's repeated insistence on 'méthode' (pp.34, 38, 43), other factors come into play which are ultimately more decisive in determining the evolution of Gertrude's education. For as soon as Gertrude begins to respond to his teaching, the pastor is deflected from his methodological rigour. Though he describes her first smile still in terms of a 'visage de statue' and with a reference to 'ses traits [qui] s'animèrent' (p.42) — direct echoes of Condillac's terminology — he himself is overwhelmed by a 'séraphique joie' and a 'ravissement' somewhat out of keeping with scientific objectivity. 'Il m'apparut que ce qui la visitait en cet instant, n'était point tant l'intelligence que l'amour' (p.42) he states, and this displacement of focus from intellectual development to the emergence of a certain sensibility hinging, among other things, on the ambiguous implications of the word 'amour', will be a crucial factor in this novel, as it was in *Les Nourritures terrestres*.

While operating on the basis that he must 'lier en faisceau quelques sensations tactiles et gustatives et ... y attacher, à la manière d'une étiquette, un son, un mot' (p.34), the pastor encounters serious difficulties in the fact that, being without sight, Gertrude is not able to distinguish those sensations which come to her from separate sources but which become improperly linked in her mind. An example of this occurs when the pastor describes her first outings. The song of the birds, which she can hear, and the warmth of the sunlight, which she can feel, seem to her to be naturally interconnected. The connection is justified in her mind by comparison with water, which 'sings' when it is heated (p.45).[9] The analogy is a false one, as the pastor points out. It is clear that in resorting thus to comparison and synaesthesia or cross-connected sense impressions as a means of understanding the implications of

---

[9] There is a misprint in the relevant passage in the Folio edition. For 'chauffer', read 'chanter'.

what she perceives, Gertrude is in constant danger of putting two and two together to make five. The pastor has a similar problem: for inherent in the teaching and learning process is the fact that in order to communicate a body of knowledge, the teacher must connect it to what the pupil already knows so that he or she can assimilate and make sense of it. This is one of the pastor's guiding principles: 'nous nous servions toujours de ce qu'elle pouvait toucher ou sentir pour expliquer ce qu'elle ne pouvait atteindre' (p.50). Analogies are of course the instrument and the embodiment of such connections. Sometimes, however, an analogy generates an aesthetic sensation over and above those sense impressions it connects together. The pastor indicates this when speaking of those analogies Gertrude finds for herself: 'elle parvint à s'exprimer d'une manière, non point enfantine, mais correcte déjà, s'aidant pour imager l'idée, et de la manière la plus inattendue pour nous et la plus plaisante, des objets qu'on venait de lui apprendre à connaître' (p.50). The pastor too, in his efforts to describe the visible world to Gertrude, draws on other sense perceptions to produce metaphors and similes of his own (see chapter 5, p.74). But the uncritical application of what is properly a poetic perception to epistemological domains where it is not valid carries certain risks. Chief among these is the fact that metaphors or analogies, whether or not they derive from a confusion of the senses, can be aesthetically satisfying, as in Baudelaire's 'Correspondances' or Rimbaud's 'Sonnet des Voyelles', without having any rational basis whatever. The story of Gertrude and the pastor shows, in fact, how sense impressions merge into aesthetic experience which overrides rational understanding. Gertrude greets the pastor's analogies with infectious enthusiasm, and invents her own with equal fervour. This, coupled with her perceptive intelligence which prompts her to sound out all the ramifications of their poetic logic, triggers off a process the pastor proves incapable of halting.

When Gertrude confuses the sound of birdsong with the sensation of sunlight on her skin, the pastor corrects her by saying the two are independent: but he perpetrates another confusion which is even more far-reaching, for he explains that the song comes from creatures 'dont il semble que l'unique fonction soit de sentir et d'exprimer l'éparse joie de la nature' (p.46). Because the birdsong sounds joyful to human ears, the logic of this statement goes, it must be an expression of a joy which is immanent in nature. We see that the pastor is assuming a connection between external nature (the sounds emitted by the birds) and subjective human experience (the expression of emotion through song). Gertrude seizes on this and makes a habit of saying 'Je suis joyeuse comme un oiseau' (p.46). The implied harmony between the physical universe of nature and the moral universe of the human imagination does not go unquestioned: if the earth is as beautiful as the human perception of birdsong suggests, asks Gertrude, why do people not speak more often about it? Sighted people do not listen so carefully to the birds, replies the pastor, enhancing the prestige of this poetic perception by suggesting that it is the prerogative of the lucky (blind) few. As for the animals which do not sing, by a specious logic he argues that the heavier and more earth-bound an animal is, the sadder it is. The nonsensical character of this reasoning is eloquent testimony to the slippery slope on which the pastor has embarked with Gertrude: but nothing daunted he goes on to assert that butterflies express their joy through the beautiful patterns on their wings. Clearly what the pastor has in mind is a utopian vision of nature as a morally harmonious entity, mirroring a perfect human nature. As Lawrence Harvey has demonstrated, this vision is of a piece with the pastor's preference for inspirational religion over formal religion, for love over law, and ignorance over knowledge (see *35*). The pastor neglects to point out, or even to notice, that the mental utopia he is constructing for Gertrude has no counterpart in reality. The poetic imagination has begun to override perception and reason.

The conversation on colour and sound is a further example of erroneous reflexes. Having presented Gertrude with the initial broad analogy between the colours of the spectrum and the instruments in an orchestra, the pastor is impressed by her response:

> Une sorte de ravissement intérieur vint dès lors rem-
> placer ses doutes:
>   "Que cela doit être beau!" répétait-elle.

Puis, tout à coup:
"Mais alors: le blanc? Je ne comprends plus à quoi
ressemble le blanc..."
Et il m'apparut aussitôt combien ma comparaison était
précaire.
"Le blanc, essayai-je pourtant de lui dire, est la limite
aiguë où tous les tons se confondent..." (p.52)

The pastor clearly sees the difficulties, as he falters in his explanations, 'silencieux, perplexe et cherchant à quelle comparaison je pourrais faire appel' (p.53). He acknowledges 'combien le monde visuel diffère du monde des sons et à quel point toute comparaison que l'on cherche à tirer de l'un pour l'autre est boiteuse' (p.54). Why then does he persist in his pursuit of these fallacious lessons?

One reason is the pleasure that Gertrude derives from the poetic certainty: her 'ravissement' communicates itself to the pastor and gradually comes to permeate his vocabulary, becoming, like 'volupté' in *Les Nourritures terrestres*, the yardstick whereby the truth of a perception is measured. He uses the word when describing — retrospectively, it should be remembered — Gertrude's first smile; he notes Gertrude's 'extase' (p.55) when listening to Beethoven's 'Pastoral Symphony', her 'ravissement' (p.69) on hearing the organ's musical harmonies and the 'exaltation' (pp.93-94) prompted by her imaginary vision of the countryside. The urge to sustain this ingenuously heightened sensibility stems from the pastor's own highly emotive state occasioned by a poetic temperament he shares with Gertrude as well as by the fact that he is increasingly enamoured of her. Hence he becomes incapable of introducing into her universe any stark reality or simple commonsense observation that may conflict with this lyrical sensation of life.

At the core of this theme is a notion which Gide has the Pastor discuss with his friend and adviser Dr Martins. The gist of Martins's argument is that the human imagination finds beauty, comfort and harmony more congenial than the qualities of the imperfect world we perceive through our senses. We would be happier in a world of our own imagining if only our sense perceptions did not constantly register the inadequacies of the real world we are compelled to inhabit. Martins concludes by recommending Dickens's novel *The Cricket on the Hearth*, in which a blind girl lives perfectly happily by virtue of being kept in ignorance about the universe around her. Reading it prompts the pastor to denounce the cultivation of such illusions, thankful that he will not need to do the same with Gertrude (pp.37-38). The irony, of course, is that he does.

The point is made most tellingly in the account of the concert at which the pastor listens with Gertrude to Beethoven's 'Pastoral Symphony' — a title which in this context has obvious ironic connotations. Here is a piece of music which sums up the pastoral vision of nature as unspoilt and inhabited by innocent, happy creatures. Of course Gertrude accepts it as a literal expression of the real world, though even she has to ask whether 'vraiment ce que vous voyez est aussi beau que cela' (p.55). This is the pastor's moment of truth, when he acknowledges to himself, but fails to admit to Gertrude, that 'ces harmonies ineffables peignaient, non point le monde tel qu'il était, mais bien tel qu'il aurait pu être sans le mal et sans le péché' (p.56). At this point the imaginary vision is clearly distinguished from the actual world in which evil and imperfections exist. However, the former once more blots out the latter in the Alpine meadows, where with the aid of the pastor's teaching, Gertrude imagines a natural idyll, complete with lilies of the field, as Christ indicates. The pastor is compelled to observe that there are no longer any lilies in the fields, since 'les cultures des hommes les ont fait disparaître' (p.91). Human agency has turned the world into something less than an earthly paradise. Nonetheless, he forces himself to share her illusion when she insists that with 'confiance' and 'amour' the landscape can be transfigured; and he listens in the conviction that her vision is more real than the landscape he sees as she sketches in her poetico-religious fantasies (pp.92-94). The thoroughness with which this theme is worked out belies Gide's subsequent dissatisfaction with the novel, a dissatisfaction prompted by his observation of blind people some years later: 'A l'abri du spectacle de tant de laideurs et de misères, ils s'évadent plus facilement dans une harmonie imaginaire, plus facilement obtenue. Je n'ai pas assez fait valoir cela, dans ma *Symphonie pastorale*' (J1, p.999, 29 Juillet 1930).

Clearly, the pastor finds it ever more difficult to disappoint Gertrude by insisting that she is mistaken. Equally, he is reluctant to point out that there are some things she simply cannot know by virtue of her physical blindness. He so admires her thirst for knowledge, her attentiveness and the speed of her progress that he cannot bring himself to risk demoralising her. There is a tragic irony in this of course: Gertrude's very insistence on clarification when she comes across something she cannot understand, her demand for an 'idée nette' (pp.53-54) on every question she encounters, are precisely what result in her becoming one of those people the pastor says she least resembles, those who 'meublent ... leur esprit de données imprécises ou fausses, par quoi tous les raisonnements ensuite se trouvent viciés' (p.53). The pastor is himself blinded to Gertrude's real needs by her blind faith in him. He offers her imprecise analogies where clear moral and intellectual notions should apply; he blurs the distinction between the real and the ideal, while proposing misleading clarifications for cases where human beings — specifically the blind girl, but the principle need not be limited to her — need rather to acknowledge epistemological and philosophical problems their imperfect senses are unable adequately to resolve.

Moreover, it has to be stressed that as the relationship between Gertrude and himself develops the pastor is less and less able to separate his function as a teacher from his feelings as a man. When Gertrude asks him if she is beautiful, the teacher cannot bring himself to say what the man is embarrassed to admit: 'Un pasteur n'a pas à s'inquiéter de la beauté des visages,' he stammers (p.59). His switch from his customary 'tu' to the 'vous' form when pressed by Gertrude to give an answer testifies eloquently to the way in which the frailty of the man seeks refuge behind the apparently disinterested, formal tones of the teacher: 'Gertrude, vous savez bien que vous êtes jolie' (p.59). That he should need to resort to such strategies indicates a troubling ambivalence in his attitude. For just as his intellectual faculties become contaminated by the unavowed feelings Gertrude inspires in him, so his need for authority as a teacher joins forces in covert ways with his nascent possessiveness as a suitor. It will be obvious, for example, to anyone who has taught or been taught, that the pastor's concern to reply convincingly, even if sometimes erroneously, to all Gertrude's questions must stem in part from his reluctance to diminish his standing as her tutor by admitting that he doesn't know all the answers.

For related reasons he finds Gertrude an ideal pupil: her blindness makes her more attentive to her teacher, unlike Charlotte who, to judge by the way her attention wanders, is clearly unimpressed by his methods — and whose education he is only too happy to neglect on that account (pp.66-67). Sometimes, however, Gertrude threatens to outstrip his capacity to remain one step ahead of her: and the words he uses to describe this aspect of their relationship indicate how unnerving he finds it. 'Ses progrès furent d'une rapidité déconcertante ... Elle me surprenait, précédant sans cesse ma pensée, la dépassant, et souvent d'un entretien à l'autre je ne reconnaissais plus mon élève' (p.66). Rather than evincing pleasure at his pupil's rapid advances, the pastor is surprised, disconcerted, bewildered, as if afraid that she may escape from his tutelage.

At the same time, while he appears to take pride in those achievements which distinguish Gertrude from 'la plupart des jeunes filles que le monde extérieur dissipe' (p.66), the pastor's comments can also be seen to betray something of the male's insecurity in the face of extrovert, independent females. The teacher's self-defensive reflexes, coupled with solicitude for his pupil's well-being, thus provide a ready disguise for the lover's possessiveness. The mask slips only slightly in the pastor's less than convincing claim to be aiding Gertrude's development when he declares: 'soucieux d'accompagner le plus possible sa pensée, je préférais qu'elle ne lût pas beaucoup — ou du moins pas beaucoup sans moi' (p.67). In the light of this remark, however, it is hardly surprising that we should eventually find him arguing that she is better off blind than she would be if she had her sight (and with it her independence) restored (pp.66-67, 109). Already, the complex of responses provoked in him by Gertrude's development barely conceals the jealousy of the lover: this eventually bursts forth when he perceives that he has a rival in his son Jacques. Again, however, it is in connection with teaching that these feelings emerge: Jacques is discovered by his father giving music lessons to Gertrude. Thus possessive love is expressed in terms of injured pedagogical pride — although the pastor has earlier admitted that his ignorance of music disqualified him as a teacher in this sphere (p.68): 'N'était-il pas étrange déjà qu'elle acceptât de lui des observations et une direction dont elle m'avait dit précédemment qu'elle préférait se passer?' (p.70). Moreover, the fact that Jacques's love for Gertrude has itself arisen from his attempts to assist with her education (pp.48-49, 70) merely underlines the importance of this problem as a theme in the novel. There is a considerable irony in the remarks the pastor uses to justify his attempts to oust this ostensibly educational rival: 'tout ce qui touche à Gertrude me tient au coeur' (p.69).

Far from following the precepts of Condillac with his statue, the pastor is transformed into a latter-day version of Pygmalion, the sculptor of Ancient Greek mythology who fell in love with a statue of his own making. (Nowadays we know this story best through the film *My Fair Lady*, which was based on Shaw's play *Pygmalion*.) So clouded is his judgement by his emotional involvement with Gertrude that ultimately the pastor is more blind to the implications of what he is doing than is Gertrude herself. Confronted by the misgivings that Gertrude expresses, he resorts to speciously authoritative declarations that blunt rational and moral awareness by means of rhetorical flourishes: 'Le mal n'est jamais dans l'amour' (p.95). Elsewhere, he simply abdicates the pedagogical responsibility he had at first taken on with such a show of commitment, arguing now that real wisdom is incommunicable and lies in becoming 'as little children': 'Le seul sourire de Gertrude m'en apprend plus là-dessus que mes leçons ne lui enseignent' (p.107). These so resemble the kind of procedures that were intended to seduce Nathanaël that we are bound to admire the consistency of Gide's critical concern for the problematic relationship between pedagogy, passion and the

temptations of contagious lyricism.There are none so blind as those
who will not see; and this emotionally-unbalanced teacher will learn
his lesson in the tragic circumstances of Gertrude's death — when it
is borne in upon him by Jacques that his most effective pedagogical
function has been to serve as a warning to others: 'c'est l'exemple de
votre erreur qui m'a guidé' (p.149).

3. 'Relire l'Evangile avec un oeil neuf'

Les Nourritures terrestres conveys the frame of mind of a man intent on celebrating his release from the restrictions of a misconceived religion. This release is marked in two ways: it is evident in the joyous discovery of all that the narrator's former religion denied him, and also in the irony — sometimes playful, sometimes bitter — with which he considers the intellectual and moral bonds which previously blocked his development and warped his sensibilities. As he looks back, he is filled with incredulity at the roundabout way in which the idea of sin permitted him to gratify a specious and masochistic taste for the spiritual by denying the basic demands of the body: 'Je châtiais allégrement ma chair, éprouvant plus de volupté dans le châtiment que dans la faute — tant je me grisais d'orgueil à ne pas pécher simplement' (p.19). In the conflict between body and soul, and the struggle to avoid sin, he has simply wasted time on notions which eventually ceased to have meaning for him:

> Je me suis fatigué, quand j'étais jeune, à suivre au loin
> les suites de mes actes et je n'étais sûr de ne plus pécher
> qu'à force de ne plus agir.
>   Puis j'écrivis: Je ne dus le salut de ma chair qu'à
> l'irrémédiable empoisonnement de mon âme. Puis je ne
> compris plus du tout ce que j'avais voulu dire par là.
>
>   Nathanaël, je ne crois plus au péché. (p.43)

He is no longer prepared to revere 'le bonheur impossible des âmes' (pp.25, 75), the pursuit of which merely debilitates humanity:

'Fièvres des jours passés, vous étiez à ma chair une mortelle usure...'
(p.25). Hence, recalling the youth he considers to have been
misspent in the service of religion, Gide parodies the conventional
act of contrition: 'Certes oui! ténébreuse fut ma jeunesse; Je m'en
repens' (p.152). This points to an important aim of *Les Nourritures
terrestres*: to subvert the inhibiting institutions of religion by defying
them, by making fun of them or by deliberately turning them to uses
contrary to those for which they were intended.

As far as the Bible, that crucial source of spiritual guidance for
the protestant, is concerned, Gide had acquired a privileged point of
view as a result of his trips to North Africa: he had actually lived in
the sort of culture which is depicted in the Scriptures. Biblical texts
take on a new meaning in the exotic, sensual atmosphere of the
oriental civilisation from which they sprang. The experience of
oriental life and traditions opens up for Gide a conception of religion
which is not incompatible with sensual delight. In Biskra, the 'rues
saintes' are the setting for sexual encounters, as the author
provocatively pointed out in a sentence, later cut, which follows 'on
forniquait sur des espèces de divans bas' (p.136) in the original
edition of *Les Nourritures* (cf.p.123; J2, pp.564-65). Therefore Gide
does not necessarily have to challenge the austere authority of the
Bible by contrasting it with his exotic dream; what he sets out to do
is highlight those elements within the Bible itself that point to a
moral and sexual liberalism directly at odds with conventional
Western Christianity. He also enlists the help of the Koran and his
favourite classics of Islamic culture such as the Arabian Nights or
the works of the Persian poets Hafiz and Saadi — works which draw
on the same sources as Holy Writ while depicting them in a
revealingly different light. In doing so, of course, Gide is merely
taking to a kind of logical conclusion the free interpretation of the
Scriptures that is the watchword of his own protestantism (see
chapter 1).

The Old Testament, that most severe repository of threats from
an implacable God, stands in particular need of re-reading. In his
'Ballade des Plus Célèbres Amants' (pp.81-82), Gide celebrates the
adultery of David and Bathsheba, and the incest of Tamar and

Amnon (II Samuel 11. 1-21 and 13. 1-29). He also evokes the love of Solomon and Balkis, the Queen of Sheba who, according to the Islamic tradition, did rather more than discuss enigmas (II Chronicles 9.1-2).[10] Alongside these appears Suleika, the embodiment of passion in Hafiz's *Divan*, who won her renown, according to the poet Jami, after having succeeded in seducing Joseph when he was the guest of her husband Potiphar — a version rather different from that given in Genesis 39. 7-15. This impertinent reworking of Biblical sources is systematically adopted with regard to the Sulamite, who appears throughout *Les Nourritures* in contexts which exploit to the extreme the allegedly allegorical sensuality of the Song of Songs in which she is the heroine: *'J'ai chanté pour vous, Sulamite, des chants tels qu'on les croit presque religieux'* (p.81), Gide writes sardonically. Similarly, the allusion to Elijah and the son of the Sunamite (II Kings 4. 18-37) in connection with a barely-disguised homosexual fantasy (p.44) shows a determination to offer a radical counter-exegesis of the Scriptures.

Such subversive commentaries, however, are only part of an attempt to undermine the entire authority of prophets and theologians. Gide makes fun of the apocalyptic visions of Saint John the Divine:

> *C'est un livre que mangea Jean à Patmos,*
> *Comme un rat; mais moi j'aime mieux les framboises.*
> *Ça lui a rempli d'amertume les entrailles*
> *Et après il a eu beaucoup de visions.* (p.32)

---

[10] Gérard de Nerval reproduces something of the uncensored version in 'Histoire de la Reine du Matin et de Soliman, Prince des Génies': see *Le Voyage en Orient*, in Gérard de Nerval, *Oeuvres complètes*, vol.II (Paris, Gallimard, Bibliothèque de la Pléiade, 1984), pp.671 ff. It seems likely that Gide draws some of the inspiration for his 'Ballade des Plus Célèbres Amants' from the poet François Villon, author of many *ballades* such as 'Ballade des Dames du temps jadis'. Indeed, in his *Testament* Villon anticipates Gide in highlighting biblical scandals: his 'Double Ballade' refers to Solomon's amorous improprieties as well as to the stories of David and Bathsheba, and Tamar and Amnon. (I am grateful to Professor W. van Emden for bringing this link to my attention.)

He mocks the sophistry of theologians — and his own erstwhile follies — in his 'Ronde des Belles Preuves de l'Existence de Dieu' (pp.41-42), saying elsewhere, 'Nathanaël, il ne faut parler de Dieu que naturellement' (p.40) and proclaiming his current straightforward tenet: 'J'ai nommé Dieu tout ce que j'aime, et... j'ai voulu tout aimer' (p.42). But for all the light-heartedness that informs so much of this satire, Gide has a real score to settle with the cruel unbending God who presided over his childhood. The memory of the torments he suffered as a result of puritanical principles drawn chiefly from the Old Testament causes him to take sides with the victims of divine prohibitions: he echoes Jeremiah's Lamentations as he cries: '*Commandements de Dieu, vous avez endolori mon âme... Vous avez entouré de murs les seules eaux pour me désaltérer*' (p.111; Lamentations 3. 7-17).

In the final analysis, Gide does not reject a God; as Catherine Savage argues (*15*, p.72), he simply wishes to exercise what for him is the essentially protestant reflex and remove the prescriptions, institutions, rituals and other obstacles erected by the self-appointed guardians of religious propriety who actually divert the individual from a true perception of the divine. Nor is Gide's aim an entirely negative one, for after the illuminating experiences he has undergone he has his own message to deliver — a message which, he maintains, is there for all to see in the Gospels, once the intervening obscurantism of Saint Paul and others is swept aside. 'L'Evangile y mène', he states in the exordium to the original text of the 'récit de Ménalque' (see chapter 1). It is therefore quite possible to read *Les Nourritures terrestres* as a Gidean New Testament. The fact is that Gide decries the harm done by earlier, misinformed readings of the Gospels. He recalls his fearful concern for salvation, prompted by an interpretation of the parable of the salt which had prevented him from really living:

> Je ne goûtais pas le sel de la terre
> Ni celui de la grande mer salée.
> Je croyais que j'étais le sel de la terre
> Et j'avais peur de perdre ma saveur.
> Le sel de la mer ne perd point sa saveur. (p.152)

The key to restrictive readings of Christ's message is, of course, the idea of a reward in Heaven for privation undergone on earth. But Gide forcefully rejects this notion: 'ce dont on se prive aujourd'hui, me lisait-on dans l'Evangile, plus tard on le retrouve au centuple... Ah! qu'ai-je à faire de plus de biens que mon désir n'en appréhende?' (p.152).

The very title *Les Nourritures terrestres* defiantly proclaims the author's refusal of a compensatory paradise in the afterlife: and the text confirms this message through its use of a convention borrowed from Persian literature. 'La Ferme', at the centre of the book, is divided into sections corresponding to the doors of various buildings around a farmyard. It is a custom among Persian poets to divide their works up into chapters headed 'Bab', or door: the intention is to link the text to the experience of paradise which, according to Muslim culture, has eight doors (see *27*, p.212). Thus Gide can be seen to be offering here his portrayal of what life might be like in paradise when the Grim Reaper has called in the harvest. The evocation connects with the epigraph (p.9), which is taken from a section of the Koran concerning the reactions of those entering paradise. The poet of 'La Ferme', however, finds that the crops gathered here are *'flétries, comme toutes les choses coupées'* (pp.102-03); he longs to return to the time when they were full of natural savour. This is no doubt why the Gidean paradise has a ninth door — an exit, through which the poet can escape to the nourishment he prefers. Furthermore, the eight books of *Les Nourritures terrestres*, which offer a reflection of the eight principal sections of 'La Ferme', underline thereby the force of the implied message that the true paradise is here, now, on earth (see *28*, p.422-25). In the context of this debunking of the idea of a paradise in the hereafter, pseudo-evangelical references such as the comments on the parable of the salt are diverted from their original meanings and become part of a general incitement to the reader to take a renewed delight in earthly pleasures. Many other elements of Gide's doctrine can be seen as similar subversive readings of the New Testament: his rejection of possessions and of cares for the morrow (Matthew 6. 25-34); his opposition to the family and appeals to the childlike among his

readers (Matthew 10. 35-37; 18. 3: see chapters 2 and 4); and the
idea of a rebirth to a new life, a 'nouvel être' (pp.26-28; John 3. 3-17;
12. 25).

Fortified by this new 'Christian' doctrine, Gide adopts an
appropriate tone to deliver it. If many Biblical references in *Les
Nourritures* have a satirical or a parodic aim, it is nonetheless the
case that in an equal number of instances Gide borrows from the
Scriptures with the intention of conferring on his book a prophetic
air in keeping with its proselytising goal. In fact, Biblical allusions
and turns of phrase flow so readily from Gide's pen that it is difficult
to distinguish between what is virtual second nature, a style absorbed
during long years' study of the Scriptures, and what is deliberately
deployed for polemical purposes. Be that as it may, the pastiche is
very much in evidence. As Bertalot says, 'Le ton de l'ouvrage est tout
empreint de religiosité; le style s'accorde à celui des grands poèmes
de l'Ancien Testament' (*3*, p.55). Space precludes an exhaustive
analysis, but one might mention in passing the notable reminiscences
of Isaiah 21. 11-12 (p.127) and of Moses and the rock of Horeb,
from Exodus 17. 6 (p.40), as well as the evocation of Elijah
mentioned above. The importance attributed to the desert, 'terre
aimée des prophètes' (p.144), recalls innumerable instances of
Biblical visionaries. Similarly, Gide uses references to the ass of
Balaam (p.29; cf. Numbers 22. 22-23), to the cave of Adullam (p.39;
cf. II Samuel, 23. 13-17), and to Saul in the desert (p.147; cf. I
Samuel, 10) as illustrative parables, and includes other parables of
his own invention such as Hylas's story (pp.85-86). Such allusions,
reinforced by a style filled with Biblical cadences — 'Car, je te le dis
en vérité, Nathanaël' (p.21) — and pastoral references —
'Nathanaël, je mettrai dans tes mains ma houlette et tu garderas mes
brebis à ton tour' (p.120) — clearly signal Gide's evangelising
fervour in appropriate terms. And as for Christ's warning about false
prophets — 'By their fruits ye shall know them' (Matthew 7. 15-20)
— Gide's rejoinder is, 'voilà le fruit de ces fleurs empestées: il est
doux' (p.155).

(ii)

As the pastor says, it is the experience of supervising Gertrude's religious instruction that has led him to 'relire l'Evangile avec un oeil neuf' (p.104). In terms of the chronology of the events he narrates, this process encompasses two phases. It begins with the early part of their relationship, recounted in the first notebook. However, a more significant evolution appears to have occurred during an important period of time about which comparatively little is actually said in the narrative apart from some brief recapitulation at the start of the second notebook (pp.101-03, 110, 117-21). This period stretches back from the present time indicated by the dates at the beginning of each diary entry (i.e. February-March), to September of the previous year, when the events of the first notebook conclude with Gertrude going to live at La Grange. We learn that the pastor has acquired the habit of visiting La Grange regularly (pp.117-18), ostensibly to continue Gertrude's initiation into religion. These details are important because they permit us to affirm that, although it is not until the 'Deuxième Cahier' of his diary that the Pastor refers explicitly to his new readings of the Gospels, this religious reappraisal is already well advanced in his mind as he writes in the 'Premier Cahier'. Indeed it is significant that as often as not when a religious issue arises in his narrative during the first part of the novel, the pastor drops the past tense of his retrospective chronicle and reverts to the present tense to set down his observations — which become thereby much more explicitly connected with his state of mind in February and March, as he writes, than with the events of two and a half years earlier which he is principally supposed to be recounting.

There is some evidence that the pastor had a tendency to bend the Scriptures for self-justification even before undertaking Gertrude's religious instruction: he tells how he invoked the parable of the lost sheep to counter Amélie's horrified reaction when he first brought home the verminous waif (p.22) — notwithstanding his declared belief that it is 'malséant d'abriter [sa] conduite derrière l'autorité du livre saint' (pp.23-24). But his later musings on this and the parable of the prodigal son, couched in the present tense, seem rather more likely to have been prompted by continuing friction on the subject of the pastor's responsibilities than by a single dispute going back two years or so: 'J'ai souvent éprouvé que la parabole de la brebis égarée reste une des plus difficiles à admettre pour certaines âmes' (pp.40-41; cf.p.61). Similarly, and again in the course of an account that is ostensibly retrospective, the pastor's criticisms of his wife's unimaginative views on the Gospels — 'Amélie n'admet pas qu'il puisse y avoir quoi que ce soit de déraisonnable ou de surraisonnable dans l'enseignement de l'Evangile' (p.22) — and of her restrictive, rule-bound type of Christianity — 'Elle regarde avec inquiétude, quand ce n'est pas avec réprobation, tout effort de l'âme qui veut voir dans le christianisme autre chose qu'une domestication des instincts' (p.64) — undeniably stem from quite recent readings of the Gospels in the inspiring company of Gertrude.

It has to be said that the validity of the pastor's broader views on the Bible is seriously called into question by the frequently self-interested and sanctimonious manner in which he invokes the Scriptures à propos of the most trivial incidents: after all, as he himself avers, quoting Luke 16. 10: 'celui qui est fidèle dans les petites choses le sera aussi dans les grandes' (p.64). Clearly, it is not a person of wholly sound religious judgement who, when recalling the most reasonable and well-founded of complaints from his wife, finds in them a pretext for forgiving the poor woman *he* has 'trespassed against' and congratulates himself on having the moral strength to be following Christ's teaching in doing so (pp. 39, 114). Small wonder that Father Poucel remonstrated with Gide for his portrayal of the pastor; and Gide's response, that he had deliberately set out to indicate 'les dangers... de la libre interprétation des Ecritures' (*OC*, XIV, p.408), should be borne in mind when we consider the pastor's Biblical exegeses.

In one sense, of course, the theological musings of the pastor have precious little to do with religion at all. They are much more profoundly symptomatic of those tricks of the mind which the pastor is, ironically enough, quite capable of diagnosing in his son's way of thinking but not in his own. The pastor accurately shows how in the case of Jacques an emotional upheaval — having to do violence to his feelings and renounce his love for Gertrude at his father's command — produces a corresponding alteration in his cast of mind and religious leanings, driving him into a rigorously disciplinarian posture: 'la contrainte qu'il a dû imposer à son coeur à présent lui paraît bonne en elle-même; il la souhaiterait voir imposer à tous' (p.111). The principle is equally applicable to the pastor. His endorsement of a Christianity familiar to readers of Les Nourritures terrestres, with its incitement to reject authority and live for the present in the pursuit of happiness and love, and without regard for practical responsibilities, is little more than an intellectual rationalisation of the emotional experiences and needs triggered within him by his relationship with Gertrude and its repercussions in other areas of his life. It is true that he does acknowledge, after the event, a certain self-deception in his early dealings with Gertrude — 'd'un entraînement j'avais fait une obligation morale, un devoir' (p.100) — but this awareness does not, in the main, extend to his religious meditations proper. The fact that they are religious, indeed, serves in his eyes to set them beyond the reach of specious rationalisations. Such delusions are treated by Gide in a manner typical of his stance on most of the opinions held by his fictional characters: he is, he argues, less interested in the validity or otherwise of what people believe than in what makes them hold certain views rather than others: 'La vérité psychologique de ces pensées par rapport à celui qui... les exprimait m'intéressait bien plus que la vérité absolue de ces pensées' (quoted in 18, pp.65-68).

Be that as it may, the questions raised by the pastor's exegeses are of far-reaching and continuing relevance — even, or perhaps especially, in a world that is increasingly described as post-Christian. La Symphonie pastorale takes up those issues raised in the lyrical ejaculations of Les Nourritures and subjects them to analysis in the context of a narrative, a form which is more appropriate to demonstrate their practical implications. The frequency of conversations on moral and religious subjects in the novel is indicative of Gide's aim to open up a critical debate around certain

key topics in his conception of religion. The problems generated by
freedom of conscience, for example, are dramatised in a particularly
telling way when the pastor discovers that Jacques wants to marry
Gertrude. It is plain for all but the pastor to see that he is jealous of
Jacques and feels threatened by his son as a rival for Gertrude's love.
'Un instinct aussi sûr que celui de la conscience m'avertissait qu'il
fallait empêcher ce mariage à tout prix' (p.77), he declares; and by
virtue of the sleight of hand implicit in the phrase 'aussi sûr que' he
manages to confer upon the impulses of his unacknowledged
jealousy the prestige of an intimation from God.

Conscience, therefore, can serve as a cover for self-interest —
but it can also serve as an instrument for avoiding having to give
rational explanations: 'A dire vrai la conscience bien plutôt que la
raison dictait ici ma conduite' (p.77). What is more, the concept
lends itself to yet another form of abuse, as when the pastor forces
Jacques to submit to his wishes by appealing to *his* conscience —
which in this instance disguises the internalised voice of authority,
the arbitrary orders of parents: 'Jacques a ceci d'excellent, qu'il suffit,
pour le retenir, de ces simples mots: "Je fais appel à ta conscience"
dont j'ai souvent usé lorsqu'il était enfant' (p.78). Later conversations
take the debate further as Jacques, chastened and in some measure
alerted to his father's state of mind by the loss of Gertrude, insists on
religious orthodoxy to counterbalance the subjective deviancy which
his father is moving towards. At this juncture the familiar opposition
is outlined between what the pastor sees as the essentially liberal
teachings of Christ on the one hand and the austere dogmatism of
Saint Paul on the other (p.105). Wilson makes a further point,
stressing that the religious debate is a pretext for evoking an urgent
ethical controversy: 'We thus see, treated on a theological level, this
central dilemma of Gide's life and of the *Symphonie*, the choice
between spontaneity and discipline, between "natural" and "moral"
man' (*41*, p.65). To the pastor, Jacques's 'C'est dans la soumission
qu'est le bonheur' (p.106) is a symptom of a feeble temperament
which needs rules to guide it and which 'n'est point sensible à
l'accent uniquement divin de la moindre parole du Christ' (p.105).
For the pastor's shift of ground from the rational to the inspirational

in religious matters is already pronounced: in his view the essential factor is a pristine sensibility untouched by sophistry and directly in contact with truths that defy reason and dogma. Love, joy, the simplicity of little children are the way to the Kingdom of Heaven (pp.106-07).

In this perspective, blindness is an advantage. John 9. 41 presents a hypothetical declaration, intended figuratively: 'Si vous étiez aveugles, vous n'auriez point de péché' (p.107); the pastor imposes a literal reading and concludes that Gertrude 'aveugle..., ne connaît point le péché' (p.108). This permits him to resolve his earlier problem concerning the gaps in Gertrude's moral education (see chapter 2) by redefining sin as 'ce qui obscurcit l'âme... ce qui s'oppose à [la] joie' (p.107). The things he could not bring himself to mention to her — evil, sin and death (p.56) — are best kept hidden, after all: to tell her of them — or 'open her eyes' to them by speaking, as Jacques would recommend, of the commandments and prescriptions in Scripture texts which warn against them — would itself be a sin.

It could be said that in this first exchange the arguments of Jacques and his father are fairly evenly balanced; essentially they represent two recognised theological and moral stances with equally respectable pedigrees. The pastor seeks to gain a definitive advantage by communicating to Jacques a quotation from Saint Paul — an attempt to turn his adversary's own weapons against him: 'Que celui qui ne mange pas ne juge pas celui qui mange, car Dieu a accueilli ce dernier' (p.111). (The choice of food as a metaphor is an apt reminder of *Les Nourritures terrestres*.) Saint Paul's words appear to deny any person the right to judge or condemn others for indulging appetites he or she disapproves of or does not share. The pastor sees here the potential for a move away from prescriptive notions of good and bad in favour of natural impulses, guided by love alone: 'la signification de ce verset est large et profonde: la restriction ne doit pas être dictée par la loi, mais par l'amour' (p.112). But Paul's words have a sting in the tail; his epistle carries a proviso over which Gide himself had agonised (see *39*, pp.67-68) and which he has Jacques send back to his father as a token of the unresolved tension between the two positions: 'Ne cause point par ton aliment la perte de celui pour lequel Christ est mort' (p.113). However, this expression of the crucial limitation on pursuing one's private inclinations — the point at which they entail misfortune for others — proves no match for the pastor's determination not to listen, to condemn this as an unnecessary complication, and to reassert his belief that 'le seul péché est ce qui attente au bonheur d'autrui' (p.113). Thus he can be seen to oppose an idyllic idea of happiness based on ignorance to Jacques's more urgent concern with the knowledge which ensures survival or salvation itself.

When the consequences of the pastor's wilful mis-understanding finally do impress themselves upon him — when Gertrude lies on her death-bed — it is too late. By now she in turn has reread, literally 'avec un oeil neuf', both the Gospels and those texts the pastor kept from her: and the pastor's religious instruction proves wholly inadequate to sustain her in her distress. Jacques, a new convert to catholicism, has read to her the severe admonitions of Saint Paul that indicate the shortcomings of his father's libertarian protestantism: 'Pour moi, étant autrefois sans loi, je vivais; mais quand le commandement vint, le péché reprit vie, et moi je mourus' (pp.145-46; Romans 7. 9-10). Where she once visualised the world in terms of love and joy, it is brutally revealed as subject to sin and death. Between these two extreme readings of the Scriptures, Gertrude can be seen as a hapless victim of the flaws in both. The author refrains from drawing any explicit doctrinal conclusions; but Gertrude's death is, in its way, a vindication of Gide's own problematic position as an instinctive admirer of Christ confronted by two unacceptable faces of Christianity (see chapter 1, p.17).

4. 'Familles, je vous hais'

(i)

Ménalque's celebrated denunciation of domesticity became an important factor in the notoriety of *Les Nourritures terrestres*. The character was seen to be issuing a challenge to conventional society. In some respects, of course, it has to be said that such opposition to the family as the book voices stems from the underlying pederastic impulse which informs Gide's outlook: in the allusions to the encounters at the school gates which are a prelude to abduction and emancipation (pp.67, 94) we may discern the fantasy of the homosexual who seeks an unattached young partner (see *16*). Certainly a special relationship such as that which existed between Ménalque and the narrator is offered as a substitute for family ties: 'Je l'aimais aussi comme un frère' (p.23), we are told. This relationship, and that which the narrator offers Nathanaël, are presented as examples of the companionship of an élite which, by implication, will supersede family ties and parental authority, and enable a child to develop naturally. But if Ménalque hates families, it is above all because they entail 'foyers clos; portes refermées; possessions jalouses du bonheur' (p.67). It is attitudes which are at stake rather than an institution. We find in *Les Nourritures* no specific attacks on parents; what references there are to the narrator's family relations before his 'rebirth' are unexceptionable (pp.26-27). It is suggested simply that the family tends to cocoon the individual, to reinforce an unhealthy inward-looking cast of mind, and to prevent or delay the all-important contact with the outside world. Hence Ménalque, we are told, teaches children 'à n'aimer plus seulement leur famille et, lentement, à la quitter' (p.23) — hardly a recipe for brusque revolt and overthrow of the family regime — and he says to Myrtil the family man: 'La meilleure partie de ton être est cloîtrée; ta femme et tes enfants, tes livres et ton étude la détiennent et te la dérobent à Dieu' (p.71).

To counter the influence of the family the narrator takes his lead from Ménalque at the outset, telling Nathanaël that his aim is to make the young man 'sortir — sortir de n'importe où, de ta ville, de ta famille, de ta chambre, de ta pensée' (p.15). Elsewhere this aim is restated with an order which carries a punning criticism of the demeure, or family abode: 'ne demeure jamais, Nathanaël (...) Rien n'est plus dangereux pour toi que ta famille, que ta chambre, que ton passé' (p.44). Here, the emphasised adjectives point to the most pernicious products of domesticity: possessions and attachments. The adventure offered in Les Nourritures terrestres is essentially an escape from such fixed perspectives into a new kind of society and a new set of intellectual and emotional postures; specific forms of thought are the chief target of Gide's criticism. To change such modes of thought, and in opposition to the sedentary existence of the majority, different modes of living are necessary, and the narrator recommends travel as the secret of true wisdom: 'Tandis que d'autres publient ou travaillent, j'ai passé trois années de voyage à oublier au contraire tout ce que j'avais appris par la tête. Cette désinstruction fut lente et difficile; elle me fut plus utile que toutes les instructions imposées par les hommes, et vraiment le commencement d'une éducation' (p.19). Leaving behind the family, the town, means leaving behind the figures of authority who dispense second-hand forms of knowledge: 'Il ne me suffit pas de lire que les sables des plages sont doux; je veux que mes pieds nus le sentent' (p.32). Ignoring the paradox involved in offering a book that denounces printed versions of experience, Les Nourritures terrestres sets out to catalogue a vast range of authentic experience; and this it does most characteristically by recourse to the format of travel notes as in books three, six and seven. These pages present a liberating journey of the mind, a 'déracinement par la tête', as Gide put it in an article rebutting Barrès's claims that the most salutary influences on the character were those of the home environment, established tradition, and the native soil (OC, II, p.441). For Gide a perpetual restlessness is the secret of a rich existence: hence the visions of the 'routes vers la plaine ... routes vers l'Orient ... routes vers le Nord' (p.37) and the repeated references to departures (pp.27, 37, 46, 89, 94, 97, 107, 127, 131 etc.). This celebration of movement, of discovery and self-discovery, is clearly the direct opposite of the stable, rooted family life. 'Je haïssais les foyers, les familles, tous lieux où l'homme pense trouver un repos', declares Ménalque (p.65), and the narrator echoes him when he says to Nathanaël: 'tu regarderas tout en passant, et tu ne t'arrêteras nulle part' (p.20). Each new landscape brings a new form of knowledge, a new vision of humanity (p.118) — but only at the cost of the traveller's refusal to become attached to any one landscape in particular. The presiding ideal becomes 'la vision de tout l'ailleurs que je souhaite': the poet dreams of other places, other lands which will permit the flowering of previously latent faculties, those '*possibilités oisives de nos êtres, en souffrance, attendant — attendant que s'attelle à vous un désir, — pour qui veut des plus belles contrées...*' (p.107).

Gide's fervent traveller develops, therefore, an openness to new experience: he becomes 'disponible' (pp.66,125), or available for whatever life may bring. The narrator leaves behind the town, with its formal intimacies and domestic comforts and proprieties: 'J'ai quitté mes vêtements de la ville qui m'obligeaient à garder trop de dignité ... Je me suis fait rôdeur pour pouvoir frôler tout ce qui rôde: je me suis épris de tendresse pour tout ce qui ne sait où se chauffer, et j'ai passionnément aimé tout ce qui vagabonde' (pp.95-96). Life on the road means being receptive to casual, unpredictable and even, perhaps, unsavoury encounters (p.39). The dispossessed vagabond — at the opposite pole from the cossetted family enclave — becomes the embodiment of the ideal Gide is preaching. Rejecting the temptations and dangers of a permanent roof over his head, the narrator proposes the wandering shepherd as a model:

> Il y a des habitations merveilleuses; dans aucune je n'ai voulu longtemps demeurer. Peur des portes qui se referment, des traquenards. Cellules qui se reclosent sur l'esprit. La vie nomade est celle des bergers. (p.120)

The figure of the nomad, constantly searching for 'de nouvelles pâtures' (p.120), is the epitome of the Gidean 'gospel', as has been pointed out earlier (see chapter 1). He stands as a repudiation of all that is settled, customary, and domestic, offering a wandering, unplanned lifestyle which is in keeping with the doctrine of 'disponibilité'.

Such is the intellectual compass of a theme which seeks to discredit conventional domesticity in the interests of a greater responsiveness to what life has to offer. But if we look closely at the way the theme is developed throughout the text, we find a rhythm which belies such an apparently straightforward rejection of one pole in favour of the other. Indisputably Books One and Two combine the excited anticipation of departure and an impatient repudiation of all that holds the traveller back. Book Three opens with an anthology of exquisite sensations culled during the voyage and develops into a celebration of nature, of all the gardens a nomad can see. But as the impressions succeed one another at increasing speed, a feeling of unease emerges which is crystallised in the description of the waves in the closing paragraphs. The 'mobilité des flots' — which are presented in some respects as an allegory of reality as a whole (see 7, pp.138-39) — makes the poet long for 'le doux port' and 'une solide jetée' (p.59): the restless movement of the journey actually provokes a nostalgia for stability. Thus an underlying pattern of departure and return, of restlessness followed by repose, can be seen to emerge, and this pattern is repeated a number of times in the course of *Les Nourritures terrestres*. The 'récit de Ménalque' in Book Four traces the cycle twice, and is followed by another departure as the narrator, wearying of the society of Ménalque's acolytes, sets out once more. But the frantic search for release that produces the 'Voyage en Diligence' is succeeded in turn by the introspective interlude of 'La Ferme' with its essentially anti-nomadic evocations of harvests and store-houses. Here an echo of Ecclesiastes in '*Il est un temps de rire — et il est un temps d'avoir ri*' (p.102) points to the cyclical rhythm which underpins the impulses the text chronicles, before once again the drive to escape stagnating immobility takes over. Book Six catalogues more exotic sights, while perhaps sketching some compromise between 'disponibilité' and stability in its references to 'une maison roulante, voyageuse' (p.121) and to the rooms, windows, balconies and watch-towers from which the world can be observed. Book Seven takes us once again to North Africa, eventually plunging into the far-flung reaches of the desert. Here, at the extreme point of remoteness and dispossession, the characteristic attraction of opposites brings about an orchestrated expression of the nostalgia for unity and stability as several of the earlier motifs are conjugated. The sands are 'mouvant comme les flots de la mer' (p.145), which echoes the unsettled perception at the end of Book Three; while the poet's cry 'Mais de la nuit, de la nuit, que dirai-je?' (p.146) is a reprise of his cry to Lyncéus at the end of Book Six (p.127). Here as on those two previous occasions the narrator seeks a fixed, whole vision, which is poetically attained through the grain of sand that crystalises 'une totalité de l'univers' (p.146). But the lyrical breakthrough is a delusion, for with Book Eight we are back in Paris, torn between the longing for rest and the call of exotic places.

Hence we find that the dynamics of Gidean fervour, as portrayed in *Les Nourritures terrestres*, are bound up with the tension between on the one hand a rebellious, outgoing quest for new pastures, for 'l'ailleurs'; and on the other hand an inward-turning rumination in which the poet savours the fruits of his wanderings in the security of a settled location (see *8*, pp.45-69). It is only at certain points in the cycle that the poet flees domesticity: at others he is happy to return to the 'campagne domestiquée' of his native Normandy (p.93).

(ii)

Much of the pastor's story hinges on his relations with his wife and children. In particular, the novel explores with considerable insight the impact Gertrude's arrival has within this family. If we are properly to appreciate the full implications of the pastor's account, however, we must consider, once again, the overlap between the chronology of the narrative and that of the narration. At the moment in February when the pastor begins his story, Gertrude is no longer living with him and his family. He has clashed with Jacques over the latter's love for the girl and with his wife over the effect Gertrude's presence has had on the household; and the blind orphan has gone to live at La Grange, the house of 'Mlle de la M..., chez qui elle habite à présent' (p.68), as the pastor notes on March 8. The clearest picture of the state of the pastor's household as he composes his first notebook emerges, in fact, from a retrospective section of the second notebook. Here we learn that since the previous autumn — that is, since the row with Jacques and Gertrude's departure for La Grange — the pastor has been in the habit of spending as much time as possible at the other house, in the company of Gertrude and Mlle de la M... (p.117). 'Quel repos, quel réconfort pour moi, chaque fois que je rentre dans la chaude atmosphère de *La Grange*, et combien il me prive si parfois il me faut rester deux ou trois jours sans y aller' (p.118), he writes. This casts a revealing light on the pastor's declaration that when he returns home after nightfall from what he alleges is 'une journée de lutte, visites aux pauvres, aux malades, aux affligés' (p.115) he is greeted by 'soucis, récriminations, tiraillements, à quoi mille fois je préférerais le froid, le vent et la pluie du dehors' (p.115). It becomes clear at this point that since the previous autumn relations in the pastor's home have become increasingly embittered as a result of the time he spends away from it; and that, furthermore, the pastor's view of his own household is coloured by the unfavourable comparison he makes between it and the comfortable gentility — not to mention the affectionate companionship — he finds at La Grange. The contrasts he draws (pp.114-20) could not be more systematic: the two households are parallel in every respect, but his own is on all points the negative of La Grange. Here the children are graceful in their dancing, there they are 'horriblement turbulents' (p.115); Mlle de la M... has 'une âme profondément religieuse, qui semble ne faire que se prêter à cette terre et n'y vivre que pour aimer' (p.118), while 'tout se fait à l'entour d'Amélie sombre et morose ... son âme émet des rayons noirs' (pp.114-15); and so on. We have here yet another juxtaposition of the ideal with the real such as frequently occurs in the novel. Of course, the pastor reveals an extraordinary bad faith in drawing up such a flagrantly one-sided set of comparisons, and above all in neglecting to indicate the contribution his own behaviour has made to souring the atmosphere in his home. Furthermore, while Mlle de la M... has three servants who 'lui épargnent toute fatigue' (p.118), poor Amélie has to endure the crotchety and none too competent Rosalie (p.115) — to say nothing of an irritable husband whose idea of helping her cope with a teething child is to advise her to let it 'hurler tout son soûl quand je ne suis point là' (p.116).

It is tempting to suggest that the pastor begins to write down his story when he does only because the snow which blocks the roads prevents him from going out on his rounds and thereby denies him the pretext for calling at La Grange as he has got into the habit of doing on his way back (cf. pp.11; 117).[11] However this may be, if the pastor's domestic situation is in such a grievous state as he commences his narrative the reader has to be wary. Much of what the pastor alleges concerning the character of his wife and children as shown by their reactions to Gertrude's arrival may well be a distortion resulting from the subsequent disruptions in the household and the comparison with life at La Grange which is constantly in the pastor's mind as he writes. Indeed, it has to be said that the novel's very structure generates ambiguity on a crucial question: was it the arrival of Gertrude alone that precipitated the deterioration in relations between the pastor and his family, or was the family already imperilled, owing to the incompatibility of the spouses and the egoism of the pastor? In other words, is Gertrude to be seen as a cause or an effect of a deep rift in the pastor's household? When for example the narrator remarks that the children, 'habitués à nos petits différends conjugaux' (p.22), leave the room when he and his wife are about to discuss Gertrude's arrival, there is a suggestion — reinforced rather than diminished by the adjective 'petits' — that their marriage was already subject to stress: but this could be a detail imagined by the pastor after the event. Such ambivalence as to the origin of marital breakdown is written into the text of the novel: it is one of the questions the novel poses quite deliberately — and to

---

[11] The function of snow, water and ice as sources of the narrative is explored by Goulet in *34*.

which the answer remains open (cf. *41*, p.38). In a key passage
pointing to the importance of the theme, a small but significant
parenthesis highlights this precise uncertainty:

> ...deux êtres, vivant somme toute de la même vie, et qui
> s'aiment, peuvent rester (ou devenir) l'un pour l'autre
> énigmatiques et emmurés; les paroles, dans ce cas, soit
> celles que nous adressons à l'autre, soit celles que l'autre
> nous adresse, sonnent plaintivement comme des coups
> de sonde pour nous avertir de la résistance de cette
> cloison séparatrice et qui, si l'on n'y veille, risque d'aller
> s'épaississant... (pp.82-83)

What is unequivocal as well as authentic is the portrayal of the
incomprehension, bitterness and spiteful recriminations which make
up the 'cloison séparatrice' between husband and wife. The
remarkable vigour with which their disputes are realised must be
counted one of the novel's qualities. Gide consistently catches the
precise note of niggling sarcasm or tight-lipped irony with which
each spouse denies a proper hearing to the other's grievances. The
barriers to communication presented by this mutual acrimony are
well illustrated in the passage evoking the pastor's return from
Neuchâtel, where he has attended a concert with Gertrude. His
resentment prevents him from seeing Amélie's point of view, while
her bitterness drives her to affect a studied unconcern which
encourages the pastor to avoid facing up to her feelings:

> Aussitôt rentrés, Amélie trouva le moyen de me faire
> sentir qu'elle désapprouvait l'emploi de ma journée. Elle
> aurait pu me le dire auparavant; mais elle nous avait
> laissés partir, Gertrude et moi, sans mot dire, selon son
> habitude de laisser faire et de se réserver ensuite le droit
> de blâmer. Du reste elle ne me fit point précisément de
> reproches ... mais elle semblait mettre une sorte
> d'affectation à ne parler que des choses les plus
> indifférentes. (pp.59-60)

Such an atmosphere where the least gesture is construed as a provocation by the other partner is bound to cloud the judgement of both; hence the pastor virtually admits that it was out of spite that he insisted on adopting Gertrude in the face of Amélie's opposition (pp.23-24). More tragic perhaps is the scene when the pastor, driven by unacknowledged jealousy of Jacques, seeks his wife's support in breaking off his son's romance. The reader can see that Amélie is well aware of what motivates her husband: but instead of responding to his enquiries with a few direct, well-chosen words which might have saved them all, she resorts to sarcastic insinuations whose very tone causes the pastor's hackles to rise, prompting him to brush aside her comments with a caustic 'Quand tu voudras que je te comprenne, tu tâcheras de t'exprimer plus clairement' (pp.83-87).

Whatever initial differences of outlook he and his wife may have had are exacerbated by the conflict over Gertrude, to the extent that the pastor unfeelingly shuts Amélie out of his life, seeing her as naturally morose (p.124), incapable of experiencing happiness (p.113), unduly obsessed by 'les soucis de la vie matérielle' (p.116) and a complete stranger to the finer realities of poetry, inspirational religion and theological speculation. Even as he experiences nostalgia for what she used to be, 'l'ange qui souriait naguère à chaque noble élan de mon coeur', he wonders whether he was not deceived in the past, so different has she become in the present (p.116). Now he sees her as nothing more than a restriction on his existence: 'Le seul plaisir que je puisse faire à Amélie, c'est de m'abstenir de faire les choses qui lui déplaisent. ...A quel point elle a déjà rétréci ma vie, c'est ce dont elle ne peut se rendre compte' (p.63). In all this, of course, the pastor's own failings are glaring enough. He condemns himself by the condescending tone he frequently adopts when speaking of his wife, like one who is striving to be fair — but who lets the strain show a little too readily: 'Ma femme est un jardin de vertus ... mais sa charité naturelle n'aime pas à être surprise' (p.19). He exploits his assumed superiority as God's instrument to override her objections and misgivings and to overlook the extent of the drudgery he leaves her to carry out unaided (pp.24,25,30). In the final analysis, while the reader may find

Amélie's character as unattractive as the pastor says it is, it is difficult to deny that her situation is more harrowing, and her judgements more sensible — and perhaps more honest — than his. Rather than apportioning blame between the two individuals, however, it might be better to read the text as an analysis of the tensions that accompany the roles traditionally conferred by the institutions of marriage and the family themselves.

From the outset, being an orphan foundling, crawling with vermin and existing in a state of 'dénuement' (p.26), Gertrude might be said to embody a form of that ideal we have seen developed in *Les Nourritures terrestres* and much prized by Gide as the antithesis of family values. Certainly the chief effect of her arrival is to test, and eventually shatter, all the pastor's links with his family. In the first instance, and this is the cause of Amélie's most consistent complaints, she supplants the pastor's children in his affections. A foretaste of this — which, given the overlapping chronology of narrative and narration, is in fact a reflection of the state their relations have reached by the time the pastor starts to write — occurs when the pastor stresses his children's muted response to Gertrude's initial appearance (p.19). It is true that Charlotte endears herself to him when (and only when) she shows her fondness for Gertrude (p.82), but even her displays of excitement (p.20) and affection (p.27) are denied any real validity: 'On les croit tendres, ils sont cajoleurs et câlins' (p.28). Gertrude's first smile fills him with a joy which none of his own children's smiles has given him (pp.41-42); and his preference for Gertrude increases as he is able to compare her docility and eagerness to learn with the inattentiveness (and, one suspects, the tendency to defy his authority) of Charlotte (p.67). Later, Gertrude's culture and grace make Sarah seem dull and uninteresting (pp.116, 119). Repeatedly the pastor's neglect of his own children is justified, and Amélie's reproaches rebutted, with specious references to the parable of the prodigal son (p.61) and the lost sheep (pp.22, 40-41) and lame excuses such as 'si j'aime beaucoup mes enfants, je n'ai jamais cru que j'eusse beaucoup à m'occuper d'eux' (p.40) or allegations that in any case his children have other things to occupy them (p.61). Meanwhile, Gertrude becomes the subject of a dispute between the pastor and Jacques which virtually annuls the relationship between father and son by making of them first rival teachers (p.49), then rivals in love. The pastor realises that his son is no longer a child but is ready to become an adult; nonetheless he exploits his paternal authority in order to reduce Jacques to 'l'enfant que j'aimais' (pp.79-80). In so doing he puts his own selfish interests above his duty as a father to consider the needs of the young man.

At the same time as Gertrude takes the place of the pastor's children, she also, of course, usurps the role that belongs to Amélie. In this case the process is more complicated, for to begin with Gertrude's presence actually triggers in the pastor a resentment of Amélie which is akin to the revolt of a child against parental authority. It is significant that as he tells how he decided to bring home the blind girl he writes: 'Dès l'enfance, combien de fois sommes-nous empêchés de faire ceci ou cela que nous voudrions faire, simplement parce que nous entendons répéter autour de nous: il ne pourra pas le faire' (p.17). This then is the first in a sequence of acts in which the pastor can be seen to be attempting to reject not so much the wife, as the *mother* in Amélie. She is the sensible, practical adult who stands as an obstacle to the discovery of a childlike spontaneity, simplicity and innocence which the pastor sees in Gertrude and which draws him to her. Thus if his own children are reluctant to enter into the spirit of their father's enterprise, it is because they are 'stylés par la mère' (p.20); and his most damning indictment of Sarah is to say that she 'ressemble à sa mère' (p.116). There are far-reaching psychological and autobiographical implications in the fact that Gide has the revolution in the pastor's outlook stem from his rejection of a mother-figure embodied in his wife (cf. chapter 1, pp.13,18). Equally, if the confrontations between Jacques and the pastor might be said to generate Oedipal overtones, it is in fact the father who would have us believe that he is the younger of the two, the true child trying to throw off the tyranny of the adult in order to develop the subversive, anti-familial reverberations of Christ's words: 'Si vous ne devenez semblables à des petits enfants, vous ne sauriez entrer dans le royaume' (p.106;

Matthew 18. 3). Although his theoretical interest in Gertrude as a little child soon gives way to a less innocent attachment, the pastor is able to use the one as a disguise for the other, as he later brings himself to admit: 'Je me persuadais que je l'aimais comme on aime un enfant infirme' (p.100).

After the awkward preliminaries to this admission — his embarrassment at Gertrude's reference, in public, to touching his cheek (p.57), his reluctance to admit that he finds her pretty (p.59), his highly suspect fear that his being alone in the chapel with her might lead to gossip (p.68) — it is the rivalry of Jacques which marks the transition in the pastor's feelings from the paternal to the carnal. In recognising that Jacques's wish to marry Gertrude reflects an adult emotion (p.76), the pastor is himself moved to see that Gertrude is no longer a child; and when both his own self-consciousness and Amélie's irony place his feelings on a par with those of Jacques (pp.82, 84, 86), it is clear that he is ready to forego not just his children but also his wife for the blind girl. By now, too, Amélie's constant bitter criticism merely serves to fuel the pastor's resentment of her and prompts comparisons between his wife and Gertrude which, however ill-founded to the detached observer, reveal that Gertrude has become a rival to Amélie as well as the children: 'Elle me fait sentir, du reste, que ce que j'admire surtout en Gertrude, c'est sa mansuétude infinie: je ne l'ai jamais entendue formuler le moindre grief contre autrui. Il est vrai que je ne lui laisse rien connaître de ce qui pourrait la blesser' (p.114).

The ideological challenge to the traditional family becomes most explicit, however, in a crucial conversation with Gertrude which occurs just before the night of the pastor's physical infidelity (assuming that is what Gide's discreet presentation hints at). Gertrude compels the pastor to admit that their love, and the children it could engender, cannot be confined within the framework of marriage and family as these are defined by 'les lois des hommes et de Dieu' (p.127). This is the culmination of that remorseless though ironic logic whereby the homeless orphan, far from being absorbed into and reinforcing the family which adopts her, actually breaks up that family and highlights the fragility of the family as an institution.

We hardly need add that this critique is not refuted by the resolution with which the novel ends: but the importance of the theme is underlined in the evocation of an ideal, holy family that occurs when the pastor kneels before the wife-mother he sought to reject and listens, like the prodigal son returning to the fold, while she recites 'Notre Père...' (p.149).

5. Form and Style

(i)

At first sight the fragmented appearance of *Les Nourritures terrestres* betokens a deliberate formlessness which would be in keeping with some of Gide's aims in writing the book. The text reproduces the disjointed character of life itself as perceived in a state of lyrical fervour by one who has come to relish its every instant. Thus no obvious hierarchy of experience is in evidence: the briefest phrase, recording a fleeting sensation or insight, gains a prominence from its isolation on the page that balances many an extended paragraph. The question of the style of *Les Nourritures terrestres* is as difficult to circumscribe as is the problem of what genre this book might be said to conform to. Its chief characteristic seems to be heterogeneity. It is written in poetry and prose — and frequently in indefinably intermediate forms. It contains portentous, lapidary formulae with a didactic purpose; it contains sections of extended narrative — the narrator's and Ménalque's autobiographics, for example — alongside impressionistic fragments set down as it were on the spur of the moment, with no concern for syntactical or narrative elaboration; it presents sometimes enigmatic notes suggestive of an intense sensation beyond the power of words to express. In places the form is that of the diary, complete with dates, locations and even times (p.118); sometimes the text reads like a scribbled, enthusiastic letter from one adolescent to another — explicitly so on one occasion (p.135). Gide's stylistic virtuosity has prompted detailed analysis from numerous critics — and his bold departures from grammatical or syntactical correctness have elicited frequent denunciations.[12]

Ménalque declares: 'J'ai, sur l'étendue sablonneuse, au soleil accablée et comme un immense sommeil — mais tant la chaleur était grande, et dans la vibration même de l'air, — j'ai senti la palpitation encore de la vie qui ne pouvait pas s'endormir, à l'horizon trembler de défaillance, à mes pieds se gonfler d'amour' (p.66). The oddness of this sentence, and the initial difficulty we might find in trying to make sense of it, stem from the fact that syntax has been subordinated to sensation. Here the subject-verb-object relationship is obliterated by an anacoluthon which unbalances the sentence and produces an impression of feverish uncertainty appropriate to the circumstances being evoked (see *1*, p.62). The punctuation breaks up the sentence, rather than highlighting its articulations, and ushers in adverbial phrases, used appositionally, which interrupt the rhythm like breathless parentheses. The phrase 'sur l'étendue sablonneuse', preceding the verb it is intended to complement, seems to attach itself by contiguity to the 'je'. The suspense created by this break in the grammatical construction is extended by the interpolation of the adnominal phrases 'au soleil accablée et comme un immense sommeil' which similarly vacillate as to the term they relate to. The deferment of meaning is further prolonged by a parenthesis in which the repeated vowel sound of 'tant... grande... dans...' is like the pulse of an incantatory rhythm, while the tortuous syntax generates assonances and rhymes ('sablonneuse/accablée', 'soleil/sommeil') whose musicality enhances the overall effect. The sentence conveys a dual movement: on the one hand it is interrupted in order that every aspect of the sensation might be included, but on the other hand, its structure is such that the parenthetical element might easily have been extended indefinitely. We are confronted by the kinds of impulse that Ménalque confesses to: the need to grasp a sensation as it goes by, coupled with the fear of letting something else escape in

---

[12] See *1*; *2*; *21*; *22*, pp.38-54; *28*; *29*. Disapproving comments will be found in Criticus, *Quatre études de 'style au microscope'* (Paris, Nouvelle Revue Critique, 1940); J. Teppe, *Sur le 'purisme' d'André Gide* (Paris, P. Clairac, 1949).

the act of seizing one particular joy (p.63). Veyrenc enunciates the principle that accounts for the impact of such writing, based as it is on interpolations, interjections and related violations of syntax:

> L'originalité de Gide, telle qu'elle s'affirme dans *Les Nourritures terrestres*, consiste en ce que le jeu des interjections aboutit chez lui à une recomposition de l'ensemble désuni, mais sur un plan de cohérence qui relève désormais non plus de la réglementation statique des modèles grammaticaux, mais de la dynamique intérieure d'un mouvement chaque fois spécifié, et qui procède des pulsions pathétiques de l'inspiration, plutôt que des impératifs de la syntaxe logique. (*25*, p.374)

Certain sentences are worth noting for their sheer beauty, to which analysis of alliterations, assonances, echoes, chiasmus and inversion adds a commentary but not an explanation (see *2*, p.114): 'Je vous ai vus, grands champs baignés de la blancheur de l'aube; lacs bleus, je me suis baigné dans vos flots — et que chaque caresse de l'air riant m'ait fait sourire, voilà ce que je ne me lasserai pas de te redire, Nathanaël' (p.23).

I would suggest that unifying features underpin this panoply of stylistic experimentation. The whole book might be seen as an adventure in lyricism, combining exoticism, incantation and ritual elements in an attempt to captivate the reader. At the outset we are confronted by a poetry which will appear strange — quotations from Hafiz followed by lines modelled on the Bismillah, or Koranic invocation of God. Books One and Two are largely given over to declarations intended to inspire a certain awe and to create an atmosphere of expectation — reminiscent of a ritual ceremony. The principal motifs here concern longing, waiting, preparations for departure, as if the reader were undergoing a process of initiation. Then come the first *notes de voyage*, exotic impressions from distant locales: but these eventually give way to a catalogue of gardens which establishes the incantatory rhythm so typical of the book. We find repeatedly from this point onwards that the particular forms evoked flow one into the other, dissolve into a flux which is whirled before the reader in frequently dizzying fashion. Here the operative stylistic features are recurrent phrases such as 'Il y a', 'J'ai vu', 'J'ai bu', 'Je te parlerai de', and sentence structures based on parallelisms, whether in verse or prose, designed to produce the effect of a litany. Springs, thirsts, beds, windows, towns, cafés, oases, deserts: we are drawn through all these in the pursuit, with the author, of an ever more intense and complete perception of the world. What sustains the intensity is a combination of two elements: one is the incantatory composition and style, but the other, equally fundamental, is a primordial refusal to be satisfied which can best be seen in the fact that Gide prefers desire to possession. Ultimately, the note of longing and expectation on which the text opens is sustained throughout: the tonality of Gide's lyricism might be described as one of perpetually-imminent but perpetually-deferred satisfaction.[13] The author said as much when he explained to a friend how he assembled the book: 'La composition était surtout: ménager la permission d'un ton toujours tendu' (5, 30, p.29). Thus the beauty of a flower 'ne vaut pour moi que comme une promesse de fruit' (p.80); the poet journeys in search of 'de nouveaux fruits pour nous donner d'autres désirs' (p.78). The text constantly celebrates all that extends beyond the present and reaches to a pleasure as yet unattained:

> Aurores, vous étiez nos plus chères délices.
> Printemps, aurores des étés!
> Printemps de tous les jours, aurores! (p.118)

Satisfaction in itself counts for less than the image one has of it. In this sense the vision that informs *Les Nourritures* is, as the narrator puts it when he prepares to escape from the relative stasis of 'La Ferme', 'la vision de tout l'ailleurs que je souhaite' (p.107). This straining after a satisfaction which must be perpetually deferred can be discerned in the tortuous structure of sentences like the ones we

---

[13] As Hytier puts it: 'La poésie de Gide est une métaphysique du désir qui tente de se transcender dans une métaphysique du dénûment, du renoncement et de l'amour' (9, p.49).

have examined: the syntax is suspended so as to perpetuate the uncertain quest after a resolution and meaning which the poet hopes will elude him. Here we touch on a point which is of some importance to contemporary literary theorists. Tzvetan Todorov has pointed out that words stand in the same relationship to the things they designate as does desire to the object of desire: it is the absence of meaning or referent which calls language into play, just as the absence of satisfaction calls desire into being.[14] Hence in *Les Nourritures terrestres* Gide engages with far-reaching issues when he elaborates a form of lyricism whose principal theme is desire and whose motifs revolve around images of objects he is cut off from. Two key moments at which this characteristic emerges most clearly are 'La Ferme' and Book Eight. 'La Ferme' begins with nostalgic backward glances at the past, at the summer which the harvests call to mind; but gradually, via the '*grains entre deux étés*' (p.105), attention turns — with equal longing — to the future: '*nous irons vers les choses*' (p.107). No significant vision of the fleeting present is possible; it can only be experienced in the physical sensation of the moment. The past, the future, 'l'ailleurs' are the stuff of literature and poetry. Book Eight, with its retrospective meditations, locates the entire text in this perspective. These pages, which begin with recollections of the narrator's 'fabuleuses promenades' (p.151), consist of a series of systematic reprises, through phrasing and motifs, of the preceding books. The tone is again one of longing: 'Oh! si le temps pouvait remonter vers sa source! et si le passé revenir!' (p.156). The narrator once more savours inaccessible joys; but gradually, here too, his attention shifts to possibilities of new departures, as he hears buses and trains set off in the hours before dawn. The book ends, of course, on an evocation of 'AUTRUI', a future tense, and an optative infinitive, all expressions of an as-yet-unrealised vision: but as we read them, we can see that they connect with the opening pages of *Les Nourritures terrestres*, thereby enclosing the entire work within the circle of ever-deferred satisfaction.

---

[14] See 'La parole selon Constant', in *Poétique de la prose* (Paris, Seuil, 1971), p.116.

Hence it can be shown that in spite of the apparent fragmentation of its form, *Les Nourritures terrestres* derives from an underlying poetic vision which is intrinsically consistent. This unity of vision is also reflected in certain compositional techniques, discussed at length by Freedman (7, pp.134-43), some of which we have already touched on. The text is arranged around numerous internal echoes, repeated motifs and recurring phrases: as Berthe Lefebvre has argued, musical patterns of 'theme and variation' ensure a sense of continuity as the work unfolds (*19*). At the same time, it is contained within an all-embracing structure based on the prologue, the envoi, and the circular pattern whereby the end of Book Eight refers back to the beginning of Book One. Other typically Gidean features highlight the book's organic form. Ménalque's story in Book Four is a 'mise en abyme' or reproduction in miniature of the narrator's adventure;[15] and another 'mise en abyme' emerges from the parallels between the eight books and the envoi of *Les Nourritures terrestres*, on the one hand, and the eight doors and the exit of 'La Ferme'. Gide's fondness for the 'mise en abyme', based on its capacity to 'établi[r]...toutes les proportions de l'ensemble' (J1, p.41), is amply justified here. It is clear therefore, that even if the writing of the fragments that were to make up the volume was, at least in part, a matter of chance, inspiration and the dictates of circumstances, the overall shape of the book has been carefully wrought.

---

[15] Gide coined the term 'mise en abyme' to refer to devices whereby 'on retrouve ... transposé, à l'échelle des personnages, le sujet même de [l'] oeuvre' (J1, p.41). It has since become a commonplace in connection with modern self-conscious fiction: see L. Dällenbach, *Le Récit spéculaire* (Paris, Seuil, 1977).

(ii)

La Symphonie pastorale also makes use of the 'mise en abyme' to underline its thematic and formal unity. The references to Beethoven's 'Pastoral Symphony' and to Dickens's *The Cricket on the Hearth* point up the outlines of the novel's principal motifs; in addition, the evocation of Laura Bridgeman both mirrors Gertrude's education, and allows Gide to compress his account of Gertrude's development while filling in the details essential to the narrative's realistic effect (see *36*, pp.34-39). The question of narrative, of course, is what distinguishes *La Symphonie pastorale* from *Les Nourritures*. While Gide classified the latter as an *oeuvre lyrique*, the former comes into that category of text which Gide called a *récit*. It is a narrative presented in the first person, and in this case the narrator is also a character within the story. What typifies Gide's *récits* is that the narrator does not see, or tell, the full story. As in *La Symphonie pastorale*, the narrator's involvement in the tale, combined with certain traits of his temperament, limits his understanding and/or his ability to paint a complete picture of events. In this sense, as Gide himself stresses, his works are ironic; they imply a point of view other than that most obviously presented by the narrator. And in being induced to look beyond the narrator's version of the story, to re-establish all the implications of what he says, the reader adopts a critical posture — which the text deliberately encourages by various means. In a comment on *La Symphonie pastorale* Gide asserted that the book constitutes a critique of 'une forme de mensonge à soi-même' (*OC*, XIII, pp.439-40). Evidence of the pastor's delusions about himself is not difficult to find; we have seen the ironic lessons that emerge from analyses of the important themes of the novel.

The technique adopted by Gide does present certain difficulties at the level where the narrator himself betrays symptoms of his shortcomings. The pastor sometimes shows himself to be so obtuse as to defy belief (see *41*, pp.22-23). When explaining how he fended off Amélie's transparent insinuations about his reasons for wanting to send Jacques away, does he really believe his remark: 'Je suis de naturel trop franc pour m'accommoder aisément du mystère' (pp.86-87)? The reader sees so clearly the implications of events the pastor misrepresents, that the extent of the latter's blindness strains credulity and seems unacceptably artificial (see *4*, p.249). Indeed, Gide seems to be aware of this problem, since he blurs the points at issue. When the pastor challenges Jacques about the latter's love for Gertrude and receives a response which is perfectly natural and defensible, he is all the more irritated. Why? 'C'est ce qui ne devait s'éclairer pour moi qu'un peu plus tard', he writes (pp.76-77). These are the words of someone who is looking back on his former delusions after having seen the light, as are his comments on Amélie's insinuations: 'Les phrases d'Amélie, qui me paraissaient alors mystérieuses, s'éclairèrent pour moi peu ensuite' (p.88). And yet, when the pastor opens and re-reads the 'Premier Cahier' after having set it aside for a number of weeks, he is moved to declare that only now have the scales fallen from his eyes:

> Aujourd'hui que j'ose appeler par son nom le sentiment
> si longtemps inavoué de mon coeur, je m'explique à
> peine comment j'ai pu jusqu'à présent m'y méprendre;
> comment certaines paroles d'Amélie, que j'ai rapportées,
> ont pu me paraître mystérieuses. (pp.99-100)

Clearly the two sets of admissions are incompatible: if the pastor had already penetrated these mysteries by the time he wrote about them in March, he can hardly make any surprising discoveries about them in April. We are confronted either with an oversight on Gide's part, or with yet another layer of bad faith in his narrator.[16]

Stylistically, Gide faces a further challenge in ceding terrain to a narrator who cannot plausibly be endowed with the literary resources of his creator. Through the medium of a dull, pedantic,

---

[16] Martin seeks to explain the inconsistency in terms of the pastor's psychology (*37*, pp.ciii-cvi), while Maillet refines the arguement to suggest the pastor has deliberately tampered with his text (*36*, pp.44-48). Babcock takes the line that such discrepancies signal the text's self-conscious character (*30*, pp.67-68).

self-righteous diarist Gide has to produce a text which will nonetheless have interest for an intelligent reader. Part of this task is fulfilled, of course, by virtue of the subtle ironies underpinning the pastor's narration, and the astringent pleasures to be derived from unravelling the fabric of his hypocrisies. But, in addition, Gide shows the pastor being moved to heights of some literary accomplishment under the influence of his repressed feelings for Gertrude. At the outset, his reminiscences of the evening when he first met her hold a nostalgic, poetic glow, as if it were then that he rediscovered his own lost youth: 'Je reconnus... un petit lac mystérieux où jeune homme j'avais été quelquefois patiner... je n'aurais plus su dire où il était et j'avais à ce point cessé d'y penser qu'il me sembla, lorsque tout à coup, dans l'enchantement rose et doré du soir, je le reconnus, ne l'avoir d'abord vu qu'en rêve' (pp.12-13). Similarly, given this poetic predisposition, he finds a striking image to convey to Gertrude the appearance of the mountains: 'A quoi les comparerai-je aujourd'hui? A la soif d'un plein jour d'été. Avant ce soir elles auront achevé de se dissoudre dans l'air' (p.90). The entire enterprise of education through analogies lends a certain charm to several of the conversations between teacher and pupil, even when such passages mainly serve to illustrate the inappropriateness of the poetic vision to physical reality. On occasions when he is especially inspired and at liberty to give free rein to his lyrical impulses, as when he recalls the prayer he formulated for Gertrude's welfare, the pastor produces sentences which are truly Gidean in their structure, rhythm and tenor: 'Hôtesse de ce corps opaque, une âme attend sans doute, emmurée, que vienne la toucher enfin quelque rayon de votre grâce, Seigneur!' (p.18). Here we can note the inversion whereby the appositional phrase precedes the 'âme' to which it relates, and the adjective 'emmurée' is made to delay the dependent clause; this breaks up the syntax in such a way that the subjunctive 'vienne', required by the expression 'attendre que', actually hovers indecisively — the more so as it is itself displaced by inversion — and suggests the subjunctive we normally associate with prayer. Such turns of phrase might be compared with lines from *Les Nourritures terrestres*. Sometimes, however, as Wilson points out, the morally dubious nature of the pastor's inspiration causes him to call up a religious motif as if to legitimise a delight of a more secular kind: a comparison likening Gertrude's first smile to dawn appearing over the Alps is modified to include a reference to the Biblical image of the 'piscine de Bethesda' (p.42; see *41*, p.29). The dramatisation of such afterthoughts is in fact an important element in Gide's use of the diary form. The diarist expresses himself spontaneously; that is a guarantee of his truthfulness. He is free, however, to add details after reflection: this too might be seen as the mark of one making a special effort to be accurate, and the reader may feel called upon to admire the writer's scruples. In the pastor's case, however, we see a subtle exploitation, to his own ends, of the diarist's supposed veracity. In this text the initial statement sometimes betrays thoughts the pastor would rather conceal, and he uses the afterthought,with the air of clarifying a detail, to deflect the reader's attention from the truth. Amélie, for example, fully approves of Jacques's having told his father of his love for Gertrude; we learn that she greets the pastor's mention of the conversation 'comme si je lui annonçais une chose toute naturelle' — which is precisely what the pastor wishes to argue it is not, so he suggests an alternative text, the innocuous 'ou plutôt comme si je ne lui apprenais rien' (p.83). We see the same mechanism at work when the pastor explains that the idea of bringing the orphan home came to him 'après que j'eus prié — ou plus exactement pendant la prière que je fis' (p.16); the impulse appears much more legitimate if it comes during prayer rather than afterwards, in a manner the pastor himself might have to accept responsibility for. He is not always so subtle or successful, of course; and Gide sometimes has him write sentences of an extraordinary awkwardness, as testimony to the tortuous nature of his self-righteousness and pedantry. The bumptiousness of his imperfect subjunctives, even allowing for the fact that they had wider currency at the time they were written than now, undermines his sanctimonious criticisms of Amélie: 'N'eût-il pas été naturel qu'elle s'informât de ce que nous avions entendu ...?' (p.60). Similarly, his attempts to defuse the full force of Amélie's reproaches merely produce a cascade of cacophonous and cumbersome constructions: '...de sorte que naturellement il lui paraissait mal séant que je consacrasse à cette oeuvre un temps qu'elle prétendait toujours qui serait mieux employé différemment' (p.40).

This *récit* is more complex than Gide's other first-person narratives in one important respect. *La Symphonie pastorale* presents not just a diary, but a diary which in part contains a retrospective re-creation of events: the imbrication of these two forms is accomplished in such a way as to generate subtle readings of story, structure and style. I have pointed out how, particularly in the 'Premier Cahier', the present state of the pastor's household — the outcome of the story he is telling — must be borne in mind if one is to appreciate his view of what he is recounting as well as the manner in which he recounts it (see chapter 4). The present of narration is shown to be crucially intertwined with the past of the story (see *11*, pp.82-85, 107-13; *30a*; *36a*, pp.138-55). This might provide an explanation for a stylistic feature which has exercised many critics: the pastor occasionally employs an unusual combination of the past historic and perfect tenses in his narrative (e.g. pp.19-21; see *11*, pp.34-48). In normal usage, the perfect tense carries with it the suggestion that the events being recounted continue to have relevance or repercussions in the present, while the past historic, the conventional tense of literary fiction, implies that the narrative concerns incidents which are over and done with, their significance a matter for detached, objective consideration. The pastor's mingling of the two might therefore be said to reflect his own ambivalence vis-à-vis the story he is telling. On the one hand he is writing it down retrospectively in order to put it behind him, to establish its significance as proof of his good intentions and testimony to his teaching methods. On the other, however, the story is not yet over; as he writes, his wife and children are alienated from him, and the life he leads between his own house and that of 'Mlle de la M... chez qui Gertrude habite à présent' (p.68) is a source of unresolved friction. Hence the perfect tense: the story the pastor tells continues to affect the present in which he tells it, as is made very clear when we come to understand the full implications of asides such as 'mon grand Jacques ..., aujourd'hui si distant, si réservé' (p.28). This comment, written on 10 February, when the pastor is tracing the beginnings of Gertrude's story, actually refers to the rivalries of the preceding August, two years after the arrival of Gertrude (for illustrative diagrams, see *36*, pp.42-43). As a result of the text's subtle composition, the reader's distrust of the narrator develops beyond a mere moral suspicion and turns into a heightened critical awareness of the workings of narrative itself. We read *La Symphonie pastorale* not just for the story and the characterisation, but for an understanding of the interconnection between story and narration, between the tale and the teller.

With the transition from the 'Premier Cahier' to the 'Deuxième Cahier', we find ourselves gradually moving into a more conventional use of the diary form, with consequences which have been explored by John Cruickshank (*31*). As the pastor's telling of the story brings him ever closer to the present in which he is writing, he has fewer and fewer opportunities to hide from the consequences of what he has done. This has a twofold effect: the focus shifts from the narrative manipulations of the first notebook to ideological or moral manipulations in the second; while at the same time the dramatic tenor of the story is heightened as events catch up with the diarist. In the first notebook the pastor could disguise an incident involving a clash of rivals in love as 'un petit fait qui a rapport à la musique' (p.67) and could discuss the practical and aesthetic advantages in being blind (pp.56, 66-67). In the second he struggles with the very definition of love (pp.127-28; 131-32), while seeking to cope with the moral and religious disquiet arising out of Gertrude's blindness (p.109; cf.*36*, pp.58-59). Meanwhile, the inexorable progress of Gertrude's awareness and of the process whereby she will regain her sight render the pastor increasingly anxious. The rising curve of tension reaches a climax at the point just before Gertrude's return from hospital when the diary notes the convergence of the story and the telling with the pastor's words 'J'écris pour user cette attente' (p.136). Thereafter the pastor is overtaken by events and the diary can only record day by day the tragic aftermath and final outcome of Gertrude's disillusionment.

6. Conclusion: Ironic Moralities and Moral Ironies

When Gide declared, 'Tous mes livres sont des livres ironiques; ce sont des livres de critique', he sought to make an exception of *Les Nourritures* (*OC*, XIII, pp.439-40). Yet there is something strangely unstable about the lyrical impulse which supposedly protects this work from irony. The very restlessness and 'disponibilité' which are the basis of the text prevent the author from being entirely carried away by his enthusiasms, as can be seen in sentences which end in 'etc. — Passons à un autre sujet' (p.125), or in statements such as : 'Je sais des jours où me répéter que deux et deux faisaient encore quatre suffisait à m'emplir d'une *certaine* béatitude... et d'autres jours où cela m'était complètement égal' (p.46).

The fact is that *Les Nourritures terrestres*, in spite of its appeals to fervour, is essentially a tentative work, conceived with the aim of exploring, rather than asserting, a certain view of life. This is clear from another of Gide's comments: 'Au temps de mes *Nourritures*..., je m'inquiétais presque uniquement de faire le tour d'une position, d'une donnée éthique, d'en faire valoir de mon mieux les harmoniques, de pousser ma proposition jusqu'à l'absurde, jusqu'à l'exténuation' (quoted in *18*, p.90).

The narrator of the book is deceptively like Gide himself, but even in this poetic manifestation, what Gide called 'l'influence du livre sur celui qui l'écrit, et pendant cette écriture même' (J1, p.40) applies. This process is revealed in the course of *Les Nourritures* by a series of features which mark a gradual shift of stance in relation to the initial premises of the enterprise. If the opening books celebrate desire and the splendour it confers on our perception of the world, by Book Four the limitations and cost of this perspective begin to emerge: 'La Ronde de tous mes désirs' denounces the moral enslavement it can lead to (pp.87-88), while the parable Hylas tells illustrates the suppression of the personality which ensues from the unfettered indulgence of the appetites (pp.85-86). This entire section of Book Four, which Gide was referring to when he spoke of 'la désagrégation du milieu', has a deliberately fragmented air; as he went on to suggest, it 'devait être balbutié' (J1, p.825) in order to convey the psychological disintegration that 'disponibilité' can lead to. By the final book, the narrator is lamenting: 'je suis peuplé' (p.151), and the circular structure of the text as a whole suggests imprisonment within a ceaseless cycle. Though Ménalque, the figure whose story is offered as a 'mise en abyme' of the narrator's itinerary, does not appear to come to grief in the same way, his prestige itself is not intended to be proof against a certain ironically debunking tone. Indeed, Gide came to regret that he had not indicated this adequately: 'Ma désapprobation partielle reste presque imperceptible et le peu d'ironie que je crus mettre dans certaines phrases ("les tableaux que ma connaissance de la peinture me permit d'acquérir à très bas prix") n'est pas assez marqué' (J1, p.1222), he wrote.

It is clear then that, as Gide puts it, 'il y a, pour qui consent à bien lire et sans parti pris, la critique du livre dans le livre lui-même, ainsi qu'il sied' (J1, p.825). But the work does more than merely set up an Aunt Sally which it proceeds to knock down again. For if the lyrical hero may urge self-immolation in the pursuit of fervour: 'Nos actes s'attachent à nous comme sa lueur au phosphore. Ils nous consument, il est vrai, mais ils nous font notre splendeur' (p.23), the chastened victim of experience reverses the emphasis and warns: 'Nos actes s'attachent à nous comme sa lueur au phosphore; ils font notre splendeur il est vrai, mais ce n'est que notre usure' (p.149). 'Autour de ces deux phrases pivote le livre,' wrote Gide in a letter of 1897. 'Elles l'expliquent alternativement, suivant qu'on le prend par le commencement ou par la fin' (5, 30, p.30). This oscillation is not the end of the story, however, for the ironies inherent in the book generate a perspective which transcends even this degree of critical awareness. Gide further observes: 'J'ai voulu... montrer qu'une grande paix, une grande sérénité pouvait être obtenue, par ce même système' (ibid.). To this end, he takes up the image of self-consuming ardour once more, in the 'Hymne en guise de conclusion':

Elle tourna les yeux vers les naissantes étoiles. —
"...Leur marche, qui nous paraît calme, est rapide et les
rend brûlantes. Leur inquiète ardeur est cause de la
violence de leur course, et leur splendeur en est l'effet.
Une intime volonté les pousse et les dirige; un zèle
exquis les brûle et les consume; c'est pour cela qu'elles
sont radieuses et belles". (p.161)

Such is the perspective of the artist, an impassive, Olympian being
who strives to see the beauty in all things and to remain, in the final
analysis, a critical though comprehensive observer. In this respect
the moral of *Les Nourritures terrestres* is best contained in the
declaration 'ASSUMER LE PLUS POSSIBLE D'HUMANITÉ, voilà la bonne
formule' (p.24). Ultimately, for Gide, the moral questions raised by
his work are merely 'une dépendance de l'esthétique' (*OC*, IV,
p.387); ethical problems furnish the substance of his writings, but 'à
vrai dire, en art, il n'y a pas de problèmes — dont l'oeuvre d'art ne
soit la suffisante solution' (*R*, p.367), as he wrote in his preface to
L'Immoraliste (1902).

However, such an impassive stance is not immediately
obvious, or available, to the average reader. Not that there were
many of those when *Les Nourritures* was first published: in eighteen
years it sold barely 1500 copies, and it was fully twenty years before
the book began to 'sortir de l'ombre'.[17] But around the time of the
First World War, its lyricism started to spread beyond a narrow
circle of initiates and was to have a marked impact on a young
generation which had seen society crumble and was looking for new
worlds to explore. Those who would later become the iconoclastic
generation of surrealists and the intellectual élite of the inter-war
years read *Les Nourritures* avidly, and for many the name of Gide
became synonymous with this work. Notable testimonies to its
impact abound (see *18*, pp.126-30; *20*, pp.240-45; *5*, 55, pp.445-47;
J2, pp.294-96): and in the heady days of 1968, seventeen years after

---

[17] See *OC*, XIII, p.443, and *18*, pp.156-57. For a detailed analysis of the
critical reception the book initially received, consult *12*, pp.201-16; *20*,
pp.232-40.

Gide's death, when revolutionary students urged their fellow-citizens: 'Prenez vos désirs pour des réalités', there were those who claimed to see in this a long-term reverberation of *Les Nourritures* — its lesson having by this time been so thoroughly absorbed that the young could view the work as faintly outmoded while faithfully reproducing its spirit.

But we have seen that the spirit of *Les Nourritures terrestres* remains ambiguous. His new readership having seen in it an invitation to pursue sensual gratification, Gide was prompted in 1926 to write a preface in which he argued that the book's most telling contribution was 'une apologie du *dénuement*' (p.12): it presents a message of austerity and self-denial rather than self-indulgence. The importance Gide attached to this aspect, and to the book's auto-critical dimension which he was repeatedly at pains to underline between the wars, can be seen in his decision to write *La Symphonie pastorale*. In this book, the hero evolves a moral stance not dissimilar to the lyrical effusiveness of *Les Nourritures*; and while Gide is far from disowning either the pastor or the pastor's ideas, he hedges both around with crucial provisos relating to the shortcomings and dangers of a doctrine based on the rejection of society and convention:

> A travers lui, plutôt encore que de chercher à exprimer ma propre pensée, j'ai peint l'écueil où pouvait mener ma propre doctrine, lorsque cette éthique n'est plus contrôlée sévèrement par un esprit critique sans cesse en éveil et peu indulgent envers soi-même. L'esprit critique, indispensable, fait ici (chez le pasteur) complètement défaut.[18]

Certainly the text engineers a number of thematic and narrative ironies which point up the manifold failures of the pastor's aspirations. As teacher, spiritual mentor, family man and would-be poetic visionary he is found wanting, as we have seen. Other ironic

---

[18] Letter to M.H. Fayer, quoted in his *Gide, Freedom and Dostoievsky* (Burlington, The Lane Press, 1946), pp.1-2.

reversals seal the pastor's defeat as the girl who, at the performance of Beethoven's 'Pastoral Symphony', was 'noyée dans l'extase' during the 'scène au bord du ruisseau' (pp.55-56), ends up literally drowning in the stream.[19] Similarly, the alternation between forms and variants of *dormir* and *réveiller* which underpins the beginning of Gertrude's wakening to life and love is echoed bleakly in the 'endormie' of the conclusion (see *32*, pp.79, 92, 259, 277-78).

If such ironies appear to arise from ambiguities inherent in words themselves, it is a fact that in many cases the pastor's misfortune stems from his misinterpretation of certain key terms. The 'esprit critique' he lacks may be taken literally, and literarily, as the capacity to interpret words in appropriate ways. Germaine Brée has argued that at a certain level the novel is a vast tissue of puns (*4*, p.247), and the Concordance of *La Symphonie pastorale* provides readily-accessible evidence to support this assertion (*32*). Indeed, in portraying a protagonist who is a victim of the slippery nature of meaning in language, Gide is anticipating the concerns of those modern critics and writers who pay particular attention to the intrinsically autonomous character of language's productive power.[20] The pastor most obviously misreads the word 'amour', failing to distinguish between spiritual charity and carnal love, 'agape' and 'eros' (see *41*, pp.32-39). At the same time, other biblical terms undergo distortions in his hands. Having established that sin is 'ce qui obscurcit l'âme', the pastor concludes that Gertrude's ignorance and naivety are a form of inner illumination. Since she is oblivious to the imperfections of the real world, argues the pastor, Gertrude is closer to Christ, 'la lumière du monde' (pp.107-08). Hence he cleaves

---

[19] The fact that Gertrude meets her death in a manner reminiscent of Ophelia in *Hamlet* points up, perhaps, another of this novel's ironic ambiguities. In Shakespeare's play Gertrude is the name of the hero's mother, while it is Ophelia he is in love with. Thus the tragic ending of *La Symphonie pastorale* reverberates with suggestions we have touched on earlier, concerning a troubling overlap between woman as lover and woman as mother-figure.

[20] For an example of this approach, see A.C. Pugh, *Simon: 'Histoire'* (London, Grant and Cutler, 1982). Maillet refers briefly to *La Symphonie* as a 'drame du langage' (*36*, pp.86-87); Goulet analyses the self-reflexive character of the writing in *34*.

to metaphorical meanings of light, darkness and related terms which fly in the face of their literal significance for a blind person. For the reader there is a higher level of irony, of course, which arises from the play on the notion of blindness (a theme which would have been underlined by Gide's original title *L'Aveugle*). The pastor readily comes to consider Gertrude's physical blindness as an advantage — and in so doing reveals the extent of his own moral blindness and spiritual benightedness, which are brought home to him at the very moment when Gertrude is preparing to recover her sight: 'Parfois il me paraît que je m'enfonce dans les ténèbres et que la vue qu'on va lui rendre m'est enlevée' (p.132).

Not that the ironies operate exclusively at the pastor's expense: indeed the essential ambiguity of the principal motifs means that the text generates dilemmas rather than resolving them. For all that the pastor fails to take sufficient account of the real world in elaborating his ideals of religion, family life, and a poetic perception of existence, his views are not without their attractions. G.W. Ireland writes: 'The pastor's failure argues nothing against the values of which he is the unhappy champion' (see *10*, pp.305-08). The debate between Jacques and his father focuses on the problems that emerge when the individual throws over safeguards and conventions in the interest of spontaneous, natural responses to life; but the debate is not brought to any conclusion. The problems raised remain on a philosophical or linguistic level, depending as they do on whether happiness is defined in terms that make it compatible with 'soumission' or whether, instead, it is taken to be fundamentally opposed to preconceived orthodoxies (pp.105-06). The matter acquires a properly ethical edge in the course of a conversation in which Gertrude manoeuvres the pastor into a perspective from where happiness stands in opposition to knowledge. Once again we confront an age-old dilemma; but Gertrude moves brusquely beyond it by declaring: 'Je ne tiens pas à être heureuse. Je préfère savoir'. She opts for knowledge at the expense of happiness on the grounds that this is the only real precaution against what she is most afraid of: 'Je voudrais être sûre de ne pas ajouter au mal' (pp.124-25).The questions the book raises become important moral issues when they engage thus with the characters' capacity to choose lucidity. In so choosing, Gertrude distinguishes herself from both Jacques and the pastor, each of whom in his own way prefers ignorance: Jacques wants blind obedience, his father blindness *tout court*. The pastor's greatest failing consists in the fact that in practice he refuses to choose: he prefers to preserve an appearance of propriety, to reconcile his inner urgings with the outward forms of his religion and responsibilities. As a result of course he travesties both and falls into the trap of hypocrisy, which is a cardinal sin for Gide. As for Gertrude, her words alone do not take us outside the circle of philosophical definitions of the terms she invokes; but what the novel's conclusion does is to explore the consequences of a particular set of actions, and invite us thereby to consider the problem in a specific case, in the sort of guise in which it presents itself with the greatest urgency.

Is Gertrude's death the necessary consequence of the pastor's actions and attitudes? 'Qu'avez-vous donc appris d'horrible? Que vous avais-je donc caché de mortel?' he asks with some reason at the disastrous outcome (p.140). We are bound to ask whether the trauma she has undergone is in itself cause for her to commit suicide. What transforms the shattering of her illusions into a fatal despair are the theological interpretations she is led to place upon the experience of recovering her sight. The pastor is to blame for encouraging her to read the Scriptures in a spirit that confuses literal with metaphorical meanings; but the letter that kills is provided by Jacques: 'Quand le commandement vint, le péché reprit vie, et moi je mourus' (pp.145-46; Romans 7. 9). Gertrude is induced to see her experience in terms of sin and death because of the over-zealousness of the Catholic convert who gives her comminatory texts to read when she is at her most vulnerable. Jacques can be seen to have suffered from a serious failure of judgement, not unlike his father, and to have contributed thereby to Gertrude's tragic end. Such dogmatic insensitivity and rigidity are, one must say in his favour, precisely what the pastor opposes in principle; though it has also to be admitted that Jacques was driven to these extremes by his father's own insensitivity. When we look at the ending of the novel, then, we see that it invites speculation as to who is responsible for Gertrude's death. Amélie must carry some of the blame for her inflexibility and her sullen refusals to intervene adequately in her family affairs; and even Gertrude, on her own admission, is guilty of failing to perceive Amélie's sadness: 'ou du moins — car je le savais bien déjà — de vous avoir laissé m'aimer quand même' (pp.143-44). All the characters have contributed in some way to the tragedy; moral responsibility is shared. In this sense it can be seen that 'l'esprit critique, indispensable' is lacking in all the characters, since all act in ways which are governed by unavowed inner impulses and rationalised as higher interests. The pastor is the most glaring example, because there is more evidence in his case; but the evidence concerning the other characters, though less comprehensive, points to similar shortcomings in their attitudes and behaviour. In the final analysis the moral point of the novel is subject, as was the case with *Les Nourritures*, to ironic shifts of perspective: it varies depending on how we view it. At the same time, this novel goes beyond the essentially solitary or solipsistic adventure dramatised in *Les Nourritures*. If the individual is seen to be still, like Nathanaël, 'pareil ... à qui suivrait pour se guider une lumière que lui-même tiendrait en sa main' (*NT*, 20), he is more clearly than ever a part of a group, contributing by his actions to an outcome for which the group as a whole is responsible. Thus *La Symphonie pastorale* points forward to Gide's next major work, *Les Faux-Monnayeurs* (1925), which will take this principle as its starting-point and will demonstrate, again using the death of an innocent adolescent as the catalyst, that 'il n'est pas d'acte, si absurde ou si préjudiciable, qui ne soit le résultat d'un concours de causes, de conjonctions et concomitances; et sans doute est-il bien peu de crimes dont la responsabilité ne puisse être partagée, et pour la réussite desquels on ne se soit mis à plusieurs — fût-ce sans le vouloir ou le savoir' (*OC*, XIII, p.55).

Select Bibliography

GENERAL STUDIES

1. Antoine, G., 'Le rôle impressif des liaisons de phrases chez André Gide', *Studia Romanica. Gedenkschrift für Eugen Lerch* (Stuttgart, Port Verlag, 1955), pp.22-81.
2. Benz, E., *André Gide et l'art d'écrire* (Paris, Messageries du livre, 1939).
3. Bertalot, E., *André Gide et l'attente de Dieu* (Paris, Minard, 1967).
4. Brée, G., *André Gide, l'insaisissable Protée* (Paris, Les Belles Lettres, 1953).
5. *Bulletin des Amis d'André Gide*. Number 30 contains important letters on *Les Nourritures* from Gide to André Ruyters; numbers 41,42 and 43 contain a dossier of reviews that appeared when *La Symphonie pastorale* was first published.
6. Delay, J., *La Jeunesse d'André Gide* (Paris, Gallimard, 1956-57, 2 vols).
7. Freedman, R., *The Lyrical Novel. Studies in Hermann Hesse, André Gide and Virginia Woolf* (Princeton, N.J., Princeton University Press, 1963), pp.119-84.
8. Freyburger, H., *L'Evolution de la disponibilité gidienne* (Paris, Nizet, 1970).
9. Hytier, J., *André Gide* (Alger, Charlot, 1946).
10. Ireland, G.W., *André Gide. A Study of his Creative Writings* (Oxford, Clarendon, 1970).
11. Maisani-Léonard, M., *André Gide ou l'ironie de l'écriture* (Montréal, Presses de l'Université de Montréal, 1976).
12. Martin, C., *La Maturité d'André Gide* (Paris, Klincksieck, 1977).
13. Moutote, D., *Le Journal de Gide et les problèmes du Moi* (Paris, Presses Universitaires de France, 1968).
14. Painter, G., *André Gide. A Critical Biography* (London, Weidenfeld and Nicolson, 1968).
15. Savage, C., *André Gide: l'évolution de sa pensée religieuse* (Paris, Nizet, 1962).

16. Steel, D., 'Gide and the conception of the bastard', *French Studies*, 17 (1963), 238-48.

16a. Walker, D.H. *André Gide* (Basingstoke and London, Macmillan, 1990).

STUDIES ON 'LES NOURRITURES TERRESTRES'

17. *André Gide 2: Sur 'Les Nourritures terrestres'*. *Revue des Lettres Modernes*, 280-284 (1971).
18. Davet, Y., *Autour des 'Nourritures terrestres'*. *Histoire d'un livre* (Paris, Gallimard, 1948).
19. Lefebvre, B., 'La composition des *Nourritures terrestres*', *Incidences*, 2 (March 1963), 23-30.
20. Martin, C., ed., *Les Nourritures terrestres et Les Nouvelles Nourritures*, extraits, avec une notice sur la vie d'André Gide, une étude des *Nourritures*, des notes, des questions et des documents (Paris, Bordas, 1971).
21. Mounin, G., 'Structure, fonction, pertinence, à propos des *Nourritures terrestres'*, *Cahiers André Gide*, 3: *Le Centenaire* (Paris, Gallimard, 1972), pp.254-64.
22. Parent, M., *Saint-John Perse et quelques devanciers. Etudes sur le poème en prose* (Paris, Klincksieck, 1960), pp.38-54.
23. Rhodes, S.A., 'The influence of Walt Whitman on André Gide', *Romanic Review*, 31 (1940), 156-71.
24. Steel, D., 'Deux textes du "Récit de Ménalque" ', *André Gide 2*, 25-34.
25. Veyrenc, M.-T., *Genèse d'un style. La phrase d'André Gide dans 'Les Nourritures terrestres'* (Paris, Nizet, 1976).
26. Vildé-Lot, I., 'André Gide et l' "art d'écrire" d'après les variantes des *Nourritures terrestres* et quelques autres oeuvres de jeunesse', *Le Français Moderne*, 28 (1960), 259-86; 29 (1961), 29-42, 121-33, 206-22.
27. Walker, D. H., 'L'Inspiration orientale des *Nourritures terrestres*', *Comparative Literature*, 26 (1974), 203-19.
28. ——, 'The dual composition of *Les Nourritures terrestres*: autour du "Récit de Ménalque" ', *French Studies*, 29 (1975), 421-33.
29. ——, 'Notes pour une étude de la composition des *Nourritures terrestres*', *Bulletin des Amis d'André Gide*, 39 (1978), 71-74.

STUDIES ON 'LA SYMPHONIE PASTORALE'

30. Babcock, A., '*La Symphonie pastorale* as self-conscious fiction', *French Forum*, 3 (1978), 65-71.

30a. Booker, J.T., 'The generic ambiguity of Gide's *La Symphonie pastorale*: reading the pastor's first *cahier*', *Symposium*, 40 (1986), 159-71.

31. Cruickshank, J., 'Gide's treatment of time in *La Symphonie pastorale*', *Essays in Criticism*, 7 (1957), 134-43.

32. Cunningham, J., and Wilson, W.D., *A Concordance of André Gide's 'La Symphonie pastorale'* (New York and London, Garland, 1978).

33. Festa-McCormick, D., 'La nostalgie de la jeunesse dans *La Symphonie pastorale*', *Rivista di Letterature Moderne e Comparate*, 30 (1977), 145-54.

34. Goulet, A., 'La figuration du procès littéraire dans l'écriture de *La Symphonie pastorale*', *André Gide 3*, *Revue des Lettres Modernes*, 331-335 (1972), 27-55.

35. Harvey, L., 'The Utopia of blindness in Gide's *Symphonie pastorale*', *Modern Philology*, 55 (1957-58), 188-97.

36. Maillet, H., *'La Symphonie pastorale' d'André Gide* (Paris, Hachette, 1975).

36a. Martens, L., *The Diary Novel* (Cambridge, Cambridge University Press, 1985), pp.138-55.

37. Martin, C., ed., *La Symphonie pastorale* d'André Gide, édition critique (Paris, Minard, 1970).

38. Moore, W.G., 'André Gide's *La Symphonie pastorale*', *French Studies*, 4 (1950), 16-26.

39. Parnell, C., 'André Gide and his *Symphonie pastorale*', *Yale French Studies*, 7 (1951), 60-71.

40. Pruner, F., *'La Symphonie pastorale' de Gide, de la tragédie vécue à la tragédie écrite* (Paris, Minard, 1964).

41. Wilson, W.D., *André Gide: 'La Symphonie pastorale'* (Basingstoke and London, Macmillan, 1971).

CRITICAL GUIDES TO FRENCH TEXTS

edited by
Roger Little, Wolfgang van Emden, David Williams

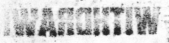

Critical Guides to French Texts

77 Gide: Les Nourritures terrestres *and* La Symphonie pastorale

Critical Guides to French Texts

EDITED BY ROGER LITTLE, WOLFGANG VAN EMDEN,
DAVID WILLIAMS